Trust Your Dog

Trust Your Dog

Police, Firefighters, and Military Officers
Talk About Their K-9 Partners

TRUE STORIES COLLECTED BY

Joan Plummer Russell

Lindholm Press

For Bob
With unending patience, he took me to
far-flung places to meet with yet another K-9 handler
who had a great story to tell. . . .

Acknowledgments

My gratitude and thanks go out to all those who helped make this book possible:

Mary and Ginger, for a million reasons.

Mary-Sibyl, Virginia, Rob, John, Sheridan, Beth, Margy, Tom, and Kate. They made suggestions and listened, and listened, and listened!

Chief of Police Walter A. Ugrinic of Shaker Heights, Ohio. Because of him my books became more than "just a dream."

Gina Gallo, author and retired Chicago Police Officer. She was severely injured on duty. She gave me solid advice and joy.

Greg Meinhard, Immigration and Customs Enforcement Officer. He gave me many introductions and helped with hidden addresses.

Each of the K-9 handlers who trusted me with their stories. Over and over I heard the words, "I just love my job."

Chiefs of Police and Sheriffs who gave me permission to ride along in the police cruisers in many cities. They must be so proud of their very professional officers.

Saint Francis de Sales, Patron Saint of Writers, and Saint Anthony, Saint of Lost Things.

My special friend Karen Klockner, who has constantly encouraged me as my agent and editor for two K-9 books. Yes, she is a dog lover.

This book has been a work of Joy.

Table of Contents

Trust Your Dog

Corporal Mike Matsik
Shaker Heights Police Department, Shaker Heights, Ohio
K-9s Drill and Aero 1

Fire Chief Virgil Murphy
Goshen Township Fire Department, Goshen, Ohio
K-9 Nitro 10

Sergeant Ray Atwood III
North Myrtle Beach Department of Public Safety
North Myrtle, South Carolina
K-9 Bravo 15

Officer Joe Veto
Solon Police Department, Solon, Ohio
K-9 Rex 19

Officer Jack Waters
Washington, D.C., Police Department, Retired
K-9 Major 24

Master Officer Todd Van Dresar
College Station Police Department, College Station, Texas
K-9 Brando 27

Officer Jimmie Davenport
Austin Police Department, Austin, Texas
K-9s Ammo and Stuka 29

Cadaver Searches

Trooper Matt Zarrella
Rhode Island State Police, Sictuate, Rhode Island
with John Turco, DVM, Rhode Island State Police Veterinarian
K-9s Hannibal, Gunner, Panzer, and Maximus 39

Captain Sandra Lesko
Firefighter Paramedic, Willoughby Hills Fire Department
Willoughby Hills, Ohio
K-9s Gondo and Eliot Ness 48

Day-to-Day Patrolling

Trooper Drew Griffith (September 22, 1961–April 15, 1996)
Maine State Police, Thomaston, Maine
K-9 Rock 57

Deputy Bob Tucker
Manatee County Sheriff's Office, Manatee County, Florida
K-9 Tessa 61

Officer Dave Crespin
Torrance Police Department, Torrance, California
K-9 Condor 65

Corporal Tim Keck
Shaker Heights Police Department, Shaker Heights, Ohio
K-9s Blitz and Argus 67

Officer Kenneth Greenleaf
Redondo Beach Police Department, Redondo Beach, California
K-9s Boris, Asko, Basko, and Valor 71

Narcotics

Detective Gene Cook
East Cleveland Police Department, East Cleveland, Ohio
K-9 Gunner 79

Detective Ed Roman
Cuyahoga County Sheriff's Office, Cleveland, Ohio
K-9 Doc 86

Tracking

Deputy Terry Fleck
El Dorado County Sheriff's Office, Placerville, California
K-9 Blazer 93

Chief Carson Sink
Astatula Police Department, Astatula, Florida
K-9 Dixi 96

Deputy Chris Stratton
Claremont County Sheriff's Office, Batavia, Ohio
K-9 Buffy 98

Sergeant Eduardo Jany
Monroe Police Department, Monroe, Washington
K-9s Jake and Chico 107

Officer Jennifer McLain
Tequesta Police Department, Tequesta, Florida
K-9s Hasso and Magnum 111

Lieutenant Tom McCaffrey
Geauga County Sheriff's Office, Chardon, Ohio
K-9s Bandit, Sheba, and Brutus 114

Constable Bradley Gillespie
Winnipeg Police Service, Winnipeg, Canada
K-9 Utah 121

Officer John Lien
Moorhead Police Department, Moorhead, Minnesota
K-9 Hickok 122

Customs and Airports

Border Patrol Agent Clayton Thomas
U.S. Border Patrol National Canine Facility, El Paso, Texas
K-9 Jacko 129

Officer Eddie Martinez
Los Angeles Airport Police, Los Angeles, California
K-9s Ralf and Marco 137

Sergeant Blair E. Lindsay
Supervisor, K-9 Unit, Los Angeles Airport Police, Los Angeles, California . . . 141

Lieutenant Guy Painter
Los Angeles Airport Police, Los Angeles, California 143

World Trade Center 9/11

Major Paul B. Morgan
U.S. Army, Retired, Jupiter, Florida/Osterville, Massachusetts
K-9 Cody Bear 151

State Park Officer John Patrick
Ohio Department of Resources, Region IV
Caesar Creek State Park and Little Miami State Park, South of Dayton, Ohio
K-9s Guese and Yogi. 155

Deputy Sergeant Gene Pence
Ashland County Sheriff's Office, Ashland, Ohio
K-9s Carlos and Ani 161

Training

Julie McHugh
Boston, Massachusetts
K-9 Training Decoy 169

Dog Handler Michael Cleverley
Ministry of Defence Guard Service, Portsmouth, England
K-9 Luger. 173

Constable Maurice (Mo) Parry
Delta Police Department, Delta, British Columbia, Canada
K-9 Decoy. 176

Andrew Rebmann
Connecticut State Police Officer, Retired, Seattle, Washington
Coauthor of *Cadaver Dog Handbook* 179

Dottie Danko
Wife of Lieutenant John Danko
Shaker Heights Police Department, Shaker Heights, Ohio 183

Robert S. Eden
Handler and Trainer, Delta Police Department
Delta, British Columbia, Canada
Author of *Dog Training for Law Enforcement* and *K-9 Officer's Manual*. 186

Author's Note

Trust Your Dog is a collection of first-person accounts by police officers about their work with K-9 partners. Today there is a great interest in all police work—the TV cameras take the public right into the scene of the action. I have shared patrol shifts with officers and their dogs for ten years. I sat in the passenger seat of cruisers holding a small tape recorder to capture these stories. I have been invited to observe many monthly training sessions and certification days. I was also invited to attend an intense two-week training session with the International Police K-9 Conference.

A K-9's main job is to protect his or her officer partner. Even a close friend of an officer cannot pound him on the back or try to hug him without finding himself flat on the ground with a growling dog on his chest. The K-9 also protects the cruiser and will bark loudly to let someone know not to come closer.

It is not easy to earn the trust of a seasoned police officer. The press has often misquoted the police. Chief of Police Walter Ugrinic of Shaker Heights, Ohio, offered to vouch for me to any other superior. My aim has been to honor these brave men and women and let them tell their stories of working with a police dog. I learned that when on patrol there may be hours of merely observing the quiet streets when suddenly the patrol escalates into a life-and-death situation. Hours and days and years of training have prepared the K-9 team to handle these moments.

When collecting these stories, I often heard three phrases: "I just love my job,"

"I have a passion for what I do as a police officer," and "Trust your dog." There are many tales of times when an officer did not trust his dog and ultimately regretted it.

I always learned something new each time I met with a K-9 team. I gained a depth of knowledge by earning the trust of the officers. I was simply fascinated by the stories they would share with me, and I think readers will be, too. Each story demonstrates the incredible depth of the bond between dog and officer.

Trust Your Dog

Corporal Mike Matsik

Shaker Heights Police Department, Shaker Heights, Ohio

K-9s DRILL AND AERO

When a prisoner needs to appear in court, he is handcuffed and taken from his jail cell. An officer accompanies him into the courtroom through a back entrance. I had been on patrol with Mike when he got the call to get the prisoner. He told me to come with him. We entered the courtroom, Mike's hand on the arm of the handcuffed man. I was walking a few steps behind them. The bailiff saw me and immediately came over to handcuff me. He must have thought that Mike had two prisoners and had forgotten to handcuff one (me). Mike turned around to see what was happening. In a quiet voice, he told the bailiff, "She is with me." During the ten years I shared training days and ride-alongs with Mike, I often heard the words, "She is with me," which got me into many places most citizens would not be allowed. All this was done with the approval of Chief of Police Walter A. Ugrinic.

When I was in the army, I knew working dogs. I worked with them overseas, and at Fort Knox we had dogs. I knew what they could do and I liked the idea of working with them. To me, it is fun. Many guys just think you put the dog in the back of a car and that's it. They do not realize the amount of work involved in being a handler.

I was a sheriff's deputy in rural Geauga County, Ohio, when I was selected to be a K-9 handler. The lieutenant had found a German shepherd at the Humane Society. He told me to take a look at the dog. The shepherd was eight months old and about eighty-five pounds. I had no idea what I was looking for. He met all the requirements: shepherd. Drill had spent his entire life outside on a run. He had no obedience training. I am told that a bond begins when you take a dog out of his cage and give him freedom. That bond happened immediately. A dog's allegiance is very strong. Dogs know no end to their love. They will stand by you no matter what.

I called my wife. "I am bringing a guest home for dinner." I did not tell her the guest was a dog. This was not what she expected! He introduced himself to her by getting on her leg. He was not housebroken, so she tied him to the microwave cart in the kitchen. He just banged it all night. Finally, she untied him; he came in and lay down by the bed. That was what he wanted. The next morning, my wife was yelling that the dog had put her shoe into a huge pile of poop in the middle of the kitchen. She thought he had eaten part of the shoe. I cleaned the shoe; he had not bitten it, just placed it in the poop. He just wanted to sleep beside me. He was housebroken in two days. Still whenever I try to hug my wife, Drill will come and sit between us.

A master trainer came from Indiana to give Drill a few tests to see how we would work together. There were two different tests. He was in heel position sitting next to me. The trainer walked right up to him. If you have a dog that cowers away from people, he isn't going to work. Drill just sat there. The trainer grabbed two pans and banged them together to make a loud noise. Drill jumped. I jumped, turned around, and gave the pans to Drill. He went over to smell them to see what they were. Those two tests showed he was inquisitive and approachable, not afraid of people. If Drill had not worked out, I would have gotten another dog. We had him at home for four months before starting dog school. I was asked if I wanted a bomb dog. I had played around with enough explosives in the army to know I did not want to be around anything that would blow up. I wanted Drill to be trained as a drug dog instead.

One of my biggest memories with Drill was an implosion. The site was Cuyahoga Heights Sewer Treatment Plant. I was working midnights when a call came in for a dog. I was told the building had imploded, blowing out all four walls, dropping the roof. The workers thought two missing men could be under the roof. I did an area search with Drill trying to use the wind to our advantage. I walked the perimeter of the building with Drill, but no alerts at all. I was looking where I was told two men were missing out of the clear blue. Drill kept straining toward a large body of water a hundred feet away. I told them my dog was not picking up anything from the roof area.

Each time I would go back to the building, he would go back to the water. I could read my dog; he was telling me something was there in the pond. Human scent will permeate water; gases rise. I asked the foreman to move the families and to drain the pond. It was twenty-five feet deep. He drained the pond until it was only four feet deep. Sure enough, the two bodies were there with their clothes all burned and charred. Wow! That was impressive! Drill had not been trained for water search, but I had been able to read his reactions. That again showed me I would have to always trust my dog. If there were mistakes, they would be mine. I had been sold on Drill before that; now I knew I had a great dog! I went back to work on my shift in Shaker. I felt good about what we had done.

A few years later, I had been vacationing in Chautauqua with my family. My son-in-law was out in his fishing boat when he saw a group of firemen. He found out they were looking for a man's body. The man had seen a young girl playing in the water. He thought she was in trouble, so he dove into the water, only to get caught in debris of branches. He never resurfaced. My son-in-law offered the firemen the use of his fishing boat, but they did not want to do that. He told me they were looking for a body in the lake. I found the man in charge and told him I was a police officer on vacation with my K-9 Aero. I told him my first dog, Drill, had found two bodies in water, so I could give it a shot with Aero. He asked what I would need. I only needed a small boat with a driver.

Aero and I got into the boat and started riding around the lake. Every time we got to a certain area, Aero wanted to go over the side of the boat. We marked that spot with a buoy. The coast guard had been called; they could do some sort of calculation to help find the body. It was too dangerous to put anyone into the lake because of all the submerged branches. That night, there was a windstorm; in the morning, a young boy was out checking his boat when he found the body. It was a quarter of a mile from where Aero alerted. Aero did pretty well. They had dog biscuits for him, and they wrote a letter back to SHPD to thank them. It had been very tough when we couldn't find the man while his mother and fiancée were helping to look.

What a dog can do is unbelievable. Only 2 percent of his work is aggression; 98 percent is use of his nose. Most of what I do is working with the dog's nose to find people, articles, and drugs. The dog looks for human scent. We were called to help locate a screwdriver in a grassy area. I commanded Drill to SEEK AND FIND. He checked the tree lawn and the front yard. At the corner of a building, he alerted by dropping his head and keeping it to the ground. The screwdriver was right there in the grass. It was needed to prove the suspect was a car thief; it was the tool he had used to peel the column to steal cars. He had tossed it when the police were chasing him. Drill alerted on the scent of the suspect on the screwdriver.

A K-9 is very protective of his handler. My aunt lived in Newbury. I stopped at her house one day while on duty. I took Drill to her house with me. Now Aunt Jean had never hugged me before, but when she saw me this time, she hugged me. Drill just ran up between us and knocked her down and was sitting on her chest looking at me. Aunt Jean's words were, "Mike! Mike! Mike!" I just looked at her and said that was what she got for hugging me.

We got a call from Cleveland Heights. They were chasing two men who had stolen clothing from Sears. The store had closed for the night. Security and police were chasing the men, but they outran them. Sergeant Jim Mariano was my permanent backup on dog calls. We met with the supervisor to learn the problem. We went to the first floor with four or five Cleveland Heights officers. Drill was carrying on; he did a quick check of the first floor and then ran up the escalator and back to the shoe department. We still did not find the men, but Drill was working and shaking and looking up in the air. I looked up and saw a vent. That's it.

We got very quiet and heard a man moving from duct to duct. A security guard told us the vent went across the whole store. That is where he was. We stacked cinder blocks and got up on top of the thirty-foot inner wall and looked down. Jimmy and I had climbed up there with flashlights, and there was the guy between the two walls. "Come out. You are under arrest." This guy was like Spiderman; he came up on all fours. He put one hand on the outer wall and one on the inner wall; he had tennis shoes on, so was able to come up just like Spiderman. I couldn't do that if I tried. The guy said, "Get your dog away and I will come down."

We kept searching. Drill kept alerting in the ladies hosiery department. We pushed out a ceiling tile and could hear the second guy in the vent shaft but couldn't find him. He was caught later. Impressive. The Sears store is huge, so this took us a while. A dog can search in two-thirds the time of a whole contingent of men. A dog can scent presence and tell us if a person is hiding behind a door or a wall. As long as my dog is telling me there is something or someone, I know something or someone is in a building by the way he alerts.

When I retired Drill, I got Aero, a black German shepherd. He was a very stubborn dog. He came from the Czech Republic. Their method is that if the dog does not respond to their training, they crank up the discipline. He must have been disciplined a lot. His reward for doing well was a tennis ball. He would lock his teeth around it, roll over on his back, and go submissive, but he would not give me the ball. I just had to wait for him to give it up.

It took me about ten days on my knees or my stomach on the floor beside him trying to get him to give me his toy. He would not do it. One day, we were playing and the ball fell out of his mouth. He looked at me and I looked at him. I got the ball before he did. I guess he thought that was the end of it, that he would not get his ball. I gave it to him and walked him out to the car. I put him in the backseat with his ball. After that, I could take the ball from him whenever I wanted, because he knew now I would give it back to him. I had built up enough trust. It was now the same with my family; they could get his ball and throw it for him. He has learned to trust us all. He knew I was not going to abuse him or hurt him and I would give his toy back to him. It did take patience and some time.

There is a yearly Safety Forces Day at Rainbow Babies and Children's Hospital in Cleveland. In the courtyard, there were firefighters, Cleveland Bike Patrol Officers, University Circle Mounted Police. I was the only K-9 handler there. The first year, I took Drill. He was a very calm dog. During a demonstration for handicapped children, one of them stuck a finger in his eye. He merely ducked his head and walked nearer to me. Drill took a liking to one little girl in a wheelchair. We would walk around the courtyard, but Drill would keep pulling me back to the little girl and sit down beside her. She told me, "Drill really likes me!" She would scratch and rub him, and the next thing I knew he was underneath her wheelchair. I kept trying to take him around to the other kids, but he wanted to go back to her and lean against the chair while she petted him. A couple of weeks later, her dad called me to let me know what a wonderful experience she had with Drill and how good it was that he was there for her.

The second year, I brought my daughter, Megan, and K-9 Aero. We went into Horvitz Tower to visit the very sick children. Aero seemed to know how to act. He would go gently into each hospital room with me. I would ask each child if they wished to pet him. If so, Aero would put his front paws on their bed, so they could rub his ears. It was a long day for him, but he stayed gentle and docile. With approval, Megan gave each child a plastic police badge, a stuffed animal, and even a whistle. One little girl told me she was afraid of such a big dog. I told her I could make him shrink. I told him to lie down. The little girl giggled. I had to hold back my own tears as I saw room after room of very sick children, even tiny little ones hooked up to an IV. When we went past the doors to isolation rooms, we saw little hands coming under the doors to reach my dog. I could only go on four floors; I was so sad to see them. It tore my heart out to see the cancer victims—so many ill children and all they wanted to do was the normal thing, to pet a dog. That year, we had access to go inside, thanks to the Hospital Chief Security Officer Jerry Jankowski, a former Shaker Heights police officer.

Another time, we had a search warrant for the home of a known drug dealer. We were clearing the house room by room. As I entered a young boy's bedroom, he suddenly sat up with his arms raised. "I don't have a gun." My God, most kids would not know how to do that. He was only seven, but well trained on what to do when a police officer would come to his house. This really bothered me. A little kid should be able to play and just be innocent. I thought that kid lives in a completely different world from where I live and work. We have taken down houses full of gang members deeply involved in drugs. They did not care if we took down their grandmother's house. The house was where they sold drugs. The lifetime of hard work the aunt or grandma had put into their home was lost because their grandkids.

Every time I make a traffic stop, I have to assume the person has a weapon. I never know what I am walking into. I do not know who this person is or what he may have just done. Even though it is just a traffic violation, I don't know if the person is wanted or is driving a stolen car. He may be on parole and now is afraid I will be sending him back to prison. Maybe he has just robbed a store. The other person in the car could have just been kidnapped. The only thing I know is that he has just crashed a stop sign, so I stopped him. A traffic stop can go from nothing into something major quickly. That is why I do certain things and ask the person also to do certain things. I need to see their hands; some will show me, and some won't. Some say I am treating them as a criminal. Then there are those who are overly cooperative. I have to watch them also. Otherwise it could give me a false sense of security. "Yes, sir. No, sir, What ever you say, sir!" When I make the traffic stop, I angle my cruiser, so that my dog can have a direct shot to come to help me. My dog watches me carefully; if the suspect begins to be loud or reaches to touch me, Aero will be right there.

Once there was a shotgun aimed at a police officer. The cop put his finger over the hole and said, "Now, you can't shoot me." The bad guy thought the barrel was plugged, so he couldn't shoot. It worked.

I do many demos for all ages. I have learned never to correct my dog just before a public demo. He will pay me back if he feels slighted. I tell the audience my dog is trained in obedience. I give a verbal command, and the dog will look at me as if to say, "I never heard that before." He just sits there without moving. I give the command a second time and he seems to say, "Huh?" So I try a hand command, and he looks at me as though I am talking in a foreign language. I start to move toward him and then he thinks, *Oh, maybe I do recognize that!* Sometimes when I am giving a talk, my dog will suddenly get bored and begin to have loud yawns and moans. Once he even rolled over on his back as if to say, "I have heard all of this before." At that point, I say it must be his turn to talk. I am really glad he cannot talk as he might tell me, "Oh, is this important to you, ah. Just you wait." I can usually tell when a K-9 gives that look that says "I don't think we are going to do this." But when they are on the money, you cannot beat them! No partner could be more loyal or more helpful.

I would never lie about K-9s. They do have physical limitations, they are not super-dogs, and they cannot run for eight hours. If the weather is 110 degrees or below zero, they can have heat prostration or they can freeze to death. I constantly train my dog. We play with his tennis ball, but I will make him lie on a cold pavement. I tell him "OK, son, if something bad happens, you have to be able to take it." I train him in every type of weather, summer heat, mud, rain, and snow. No matter the conditions, so he will be well trained. All dogs need positive reinforcement, just as humans do. If they are constantly corrected, it has to affect them. I always praise him with GOOD DOG! said over and over while I stroke his back.

If he has done something incorrectly, I will give the command a second time. If he obeys, he will raise his paw for me; if I grab the paw, he knows he has done well.

An elderly Notre Dame nun had walked out of the convent wearing only slippers and a nightgown. When she was missed, the nuns called 911. She had been missing about fifteen minutes when we were called. Drill sniffed a piece of her clothing and began a track. It was snowing, so we could see her footprints, but I kept losing the visual part. Drill kept tracking. She had wandered onto a road and back into the snow. When Drill found her, she was sitting on a guardrail over a bridge. It took us twenty minutes to find her. A warm police car came to take her back to the convent. The nuns wanted to give us cookies and milk. But being there in the convent, I suddenly remembered being smacked around by nuns when I was young. So I just said, that was OK. I wanted to get out of there. Thank you, Sisters, and good-bye.

The death of a sixteen-year-old girl was probably the saddest case I had. It was late at night. A person called 911 to say he heard a scream in the vicinity of his home. We were dispatched to the area. Nothing was seen or found. I was then dispatched to the other end of the city for another call. Fifteen minutes later, after finishing the second call, I was dispatched to the same area where the scream had been heard along with two other officers. We were told that the girl's boyfriend had found her bicycle but could not find her. The boyfriend was a teenager. He showed us where he found the bicycle in the hedges about a foot from the sidewalk. The hedges were tall and six feet wide.

I got K-9 Drill, so we could begin a track. I took him to the bicycle, and from there the track went to an intersection; we turned right and Drill lost the scent. We checked the entire intersection. But Drill showed no indications of relocating the track. I took him back to the intersection and worked him in the entire area. He showed no indications of relocating the track. I thought she may have gotten into a car or the scent had been blown away by the traffic in the street.

The two officers and I walked back up the driveway where the bicycle was found. We came through the yard and onto the patio and began searching the area with our flashlights. We saw her body lying on the lawn next to the hedges. I felt sad seeing her there. It hit home because

I have daughters about the same age as the victim. Then my training kicked in. It was time to be a policeman and do my job. This was a crime scene, and we needed to treat it as one. We didn't want to make a mistake that could result in the person getting away with the crime. We checked immediately for vital signs. There were none. One officer stayed with the girl; the other officer and I got our crime scene equipment. I put Drill back in my cruiser and began thinking about what needed to be done. The scene was taped off to preserve it for the detectives. When I saw the condition of the body, I felt sadness because she was so young. I had to put that sadness behind me as I went to work—so the person responsible would be caught.

Fire Chief Virgil Murphy

Goshen Township Fire Department, Goshen, Ohio
K-9 NITRO

I met Virgil for early breakfast, and I listened until the lunch crowd appeared. To look at Virgil, you would see a very seasoned, confident fire chief who loves his job. There were a few tears on his face as he told me about losing his beloved K-9 Nitro. I learned many things an arsonist might like to know, but will not hear from me.

I first became interested in obtaining an arson dog when I read about the first arson dog in the United States: a Connecticut State Police K-9, Mattie. At that time, we were having a lot of arson fires. Some were labeled accidental, such as discarded cigarettes or electrical. But we really knew there was something wrong. We could not pinpoint it, as we were young and dumb. Our organization of fire chiefs and firefighters was about five years old when K-9 Nitro was added.

I am the arson investigator for my department, and Nitro became the first arson dog in Ohio. We slowly became a team. It took time for me to learn to always trust my dog. To introduce a new substance to him, I would put a drop of material full-strength on a tennis ball. Then we would play fetch. I would begin to dilute the scent until Nitro could pick up the scent when it was 98 percent destroyed. He learned to scent eighteen different materials, among them gasoline, kerosene, diesel fuel, alcohol, rubbing alcohol, straight alcohol, and denatured alcohol. Some of the fastest evaporating substances are probably the hardest for a dog to get. People breathe in parts per million; dogs can breathe in parts per billion. I had to be careful. I did not want to burn out his nose. If there was a fire with a very strong odor, I would refuse to put him in the building. My guideline was that I would not send him in if it irritated my eyes or senses. I had to protect my dog. Not that he wouldn't go to work, but that would not be fair to him. If I can smell it, I don't need him to tell me it is there. Believe me: I have made my mistakes with him. A couple of times I did not trust my dog, and it cost me.

Most fires are spontaneous. Right now, we seem to have a handle on arson fires. They still do happen. We have put people in jail, and we do keep a tight rein on this. When we find an arsonist, we make a big deal out of it. The local papers also play it up to warn would-be arsonists. We do get good press. K-9 Nitro was featured on the front page with the caption, "The Nose Knows."

A fire! As the trucks rolled in some of the family were outside the building screaming that their children were inside. A firefighter ran into the house and was able to hand out one of the children. He went back inside and found the baby in the crib among dozens of stuffed animals. The firefighter took off his mask and put it on the baby's face. The baby had died. I tried to take the baby away from him, but I saw the look on his face. He could not let go. I had to physically force his fingers off the baby. If only the public could know the reaction of a firefighter when faced with the death of an innocent one.

There was an attempted firebombing of a car. The Molotov cocktail was lying right out in plain sight. It was made up of gasoline in some type of liquid detergent. Instead of splashing when thrown it sticks and runs down. Being the brilliant one, I pre-scented a tennis ball with gasoline and gave Nitro the command SMOKE. He ran to the Molotov cocktail and acted as though it was not there. I was thinking what on earth was going on! I put him back into my truck and pre-scented the ball with diesel fuel, gave him his alert, and again he ignored the bottle. There was a police officer nearby who had heard my stories about how great Nitro was. I am thinking, *How in hell do I get out of this?* I went over to the container, touched it, and smelled my fingers. It had kind of a lacquer thinner smell to it. I pre-scented that, and Nitro hit right on the Molotov cocktail right away. I learned a valuable lesson that day. If I was not sure of the material, I would not present him; he would only hit on what I had pre-scented, and nothing else mattered to him.

Nitro was cross-trained in cadaver work with a different set of commands. We have worked several fires that contained dead bodies, but he never paid attention. His command had been for arson and he did what I had commanded him to do.

One time, thirty-five firefighters were working a fire that had twenty-seven dead sheep. Nitro ignored them. He began to track two kids who had run from the scene. Nitro ran across the field to a fence. I yelled at him to get back on track. That was almost a mistake on my part. Someone had seen a man carrying a red object running from the scene. That was my focus. I yelled at Nitro to keep tracking the man. His attitude got crappy. I called him back to the fire site. Nitro again ran across the field to the same hole in the fence. He began tracking. I decided to let him go and I am glad I did. He ran a fourth of a mile right to the front door of the kids' house. The next morning, the parents called the police to talk to the boys. The police got a confession from them. I learned again to trust my dog.

We got a call for a mobile home fire with entrapment. An elderly lady in a wheelchair was inside. That always sends chills down my spine. Luckily, the fire was on the porch and had burned itself out. The lady was so afraid, she would not open the door for us. We finally convinced her we were from the fire department. It seems she and her grandson had an argument. She told him to leave. He set the fire on the porch. I do not like arsonists; if they do the crime, they must pay. He said he had not done it. Grandma said he was lying. I told him I believed his grandma and would ask him one more time if he had set the fire. I took K-9 Nitro from my truck. He immediately hit on the empty gasoline can. I then asked several people from the neighborhood to line up. I took Nitro down behind the row of men. Nitro alerted by sitting down behind the boy. I did it a second time. This time, the boy had his hand in his pocket. Nitro again alerted on him and nudged the boy's pocket. I did not acknowledge or say anything. Nitro had told me all I needed to know.

A police officer accompanied me when I told the boy that my dog had told me who set the fire. I asked him if he wondered why Nitro had nudged the pocket. The boy replied that he thought the dog was going to bite him. He did not know Nitro does not have any aggression in him. I told the boy he had touched the gasoline container with his hand. That can had not had fresh gas in it for over eight months; there was just enough in the bottom of the can to light a fire. We got a full confession from him. He did eighteen months in jail.

We had another reported mobile home fire. The lady next door to the fire had seen two young kids run from the scene. It was evident that the fuel used was charcoal lighter fluid. I did not have to present Nitro. Not only did he pick up the scent of the flammable liquid, but also the scent of the children. He took off tracking them. On the way, we passed a shallow pond about three feet deep. Nitro jumped in and ducked his head below the water. I thought he had found a cadaver. I got him out and back on the track. He took two steps and jumped back into the pond. I asked the police officer to stay by the pond and not to let anyone come near it. This park had 450 mobile homes. Nitro went right to one porch and sat down. The mother came to the door, I told her, "My dog had just told me that someone involved in setting a fire had come to this house." She said her boys were home, but they wouldn't do anything like that. Right, lady! We got a confession in twenty minutes from boys ages eight and nine.

I returned to the pond with a rake. What in hell could be in this pond? I caught a bag of marijuana on the rake. Nitro had originally been trained in drug detection. I shook my head. My dog kept teaching me new things. In the middle of a track, he had been able to scent marijuana in a pond!

Nitro and I had been working together for less than a year when there was a case of a fire set on the second floor of a building. Nitro has never liked stairs and would only go up if I continued to coax him. When we got to the landing, he did not want to continue. I forced him. It had been a heavy burn. I went four feet into the room when the floor began to collapse. Nitro jumped out of the window. I had him on a thirteen-foot lead attached to his collar. I was now standing on the floor studs. I was screaming to the guys outside to grab Nitro as he was being choked as he hung from the window. From then on, when I took him into a building, he did not wear a collar. And if he refused to go, I did not urge him. Again, I had not trusted my dog.

A fire does not care if you are male or female. It just knows one thing: to destroy. Many people think that you can contain fire, that you can control it with the right technique. This is not a big tech thing; it is a basic principle. You put the wet stuff on the red stuff. If you do it properly, the fire dies. I take that as a personal challenge. I do not have glamour stories to tell. Most of a firefighter's work is down and dirty and sometimes very sad.

We did a search for a young child who had been incinerated. His body was found in a land dump. So very sad. It was amazing that we were on a four-hundred-foot mound covering three-and-a-half acres. Luckily, when the city incinerates, we know what area of the city they had worked that day. That gave us a narrow area to search. Other handlers with three dogs joined us. I carried little flags to put on each spot where a dog had alerted. The mother had reported her child missing from their apartment. She later finally confessed. We learned she had drowned him in the bathtub and then put him in a Dumpster. That is how we knew where to look for the child. When it comes to small children, that is the very hardest for all of us to deal with.

Sergeant Ray Atwood III

North Myrtle Beach Department of Public Safety
North Myrtle, South Carolina
K-9 Bravo

It is difficult for me to introduce Ray to my readers because so many incidents come to mind from the three years of ride-alongs with him and Bravo. There was to be a SWAT raid on a drug house. The plan seemed very thorough and I was excited to be included. The SWAT team gained entrance with a battering ram. Several people were arrested, but much of that was out of my sight. Bravo would not go inside to sniff for drugs until all the rooms were cleared of anything that might injure him. There was a lot of loud talking. Neighbors were asking me questions as though I was part of the operation. As all of this unfolded, I thought: This is not a plot from Law and Order; *this is the real thing and I am here. Ray comes from a law enforcement family. His grandfather was a chief deputy who retired after fifty years as a sworn officer. Ray's dad also worked in law enforcement. Ray's brother, Brent, is also a handler with K-9 Jorge.*

When I first started working with Bravo, I found it really hard to trust his nose. I learned my trust-your-dog lesson through a Customs K-9 trainer with twenty years' experience. He had taken a two-by-four board, split it down the middle, hollowed it out, placed some dope inside, then sealed it closed. It looked like a piece of scrap wood. He placed it in the bottom of a crate and anchored it in place. We were doing an open area search in a storage area when suddenly Bravo jumped into the empty crate. He pawed until he pried up the piece of board. I took it from him and he still tried to play with it. I took it again and told him to FIND IT (meaning the dope). He kept getting the board, and I kept taking it away until he finally just sat down and smirked at me. The trainer said I should think about what my dog had done. I said, "He is trying to dig up the rocks."

He said, "Trust your dog. What did he do?" I suddenly realized that Bravo had given me the wood three times. Oops! That is how I learned to trust my dog!

Although I have always loved my job, I felt more complete as an officer when I became a handler with K-9 Bravo. We are police officers; Bravo is also an officer, just like me, and when we go on patrol, he must be alert to criminal activities just like me. Bravo's training has made him an expert in drug detection; I reply on his expertise. I may overlook things, but Bravo never does. When he alerts on a vehicle, I know there is probable cause for a search. When we have the opportunity, Bravo and I like to work with DEA (Drug Enforcement Agents) and Customs officers. We are called to search the shrimp trawlers for drugs. Although we have located the "hiding places" for drugs, they have already been removed for drops or thrown overboard by the time we search.

Sometimes Bravo and I are called out for tracking. It could be a robbery suspect or a lost child. Either way, I do my best to establish the track. Although our main training is in drug detection, we feel a real urgency when we are asked to assist on a track, especially when searching for a lost child.

Training is very important with K-9s. We hold regular training days here or in Wilmington, North Carolina. We have trained on the Battleship *North Carolina,* so the K-9s will be familiar with searching in various environments. Ships can create particular problems for our dogs. The engine rooms are extremely loud and can have fuel spills on the deck. I will not subject Bravo to any dangerous situations. No amount of "dope" on a ship is worth endangering my K-9 partner.

There are many places that drugs can be hidden on these trawlers. Sometimes they are packed in with the fish or hidden in secret compartments. If Bravo alerts, I know the drugs were there at one time. He will alert even if the drugs have been removed. He is sensitive to even a trace.

One of my responsibilities to my dog is to check to make sure the search area is safe for him to enter. He is my partner. We look out for each other, so we both can go home at the end our shift. I remember one Memorial Day weekend. We were walking through a parking lot when Bravo jerked me over to a car with a couple of guys inside. Bravo pounced on the car door and was scratching frantically. One guy asked me what was the matter with my dog—and what was he doing to the car? I told him it is called a positive alert. That means my dog has found a presence of drug odor in the car. The guy told me he had nothing in the car. I said I guessed that meant he wouldn't mind if I looked inside. Then he asked what right I would have to do that. I told him that when my K-9 partner alerts, it gives me probable cause for a search and they would need to exit the vehicle. Wouldn't you know? All of a sudden, the car did not belong to him. The real owner had just walked away. I said that was too bad, because the one sitting in the driver's seat with the key in the ignition was considered in control of the vehicle, and that would be him. Bravo recovered forty grams of marijuana, found in the driver's door. The guy went to jail.

We were walking in our neighborhood one evening. We were at the lake when Bravo pulled me toward the bridge. He was digging and growling. I looked. There was a Baggie of marijuana, a pipe, and a measuring scale. Way to go, Bravo! Good job!

A few firefighters tried to fool us. They hid some "dope" in an empty coffee can, refilled it with coffee, and put it in a cabinet. Although Bravo and I had not worked with "masked odors," I accepted their challenge. Sure enough, Bravo alerted on the can. I rewarded Bravo with a game of tug-of-war with a knotted towel.

Early one morning, Bravo and I were on standby while the service of a narcotic warrant was being conducted. The bottom floor was unsafe for Bravo, so he was deployed to the upstairs area. He alerted on the defendant's pants, lying on the floor, in front of the closet. Those pants contained approximately $718. He alerted inside the closet; a black drawstring bag was retrieved with approximately 128 grams of white powder thought to be cocaine. He then alerted on shoes. One pair contained $2,055. The other pair had a loaded 38-caliber two-shot Derringer. The field tests found substances positive for marijuana and/or cocaine. Another job well done, Bravo!

On an assist with Myrtle Beach narcotics officers, we engaged in a search of a local motel for drug activities. The search revealed marijuana, with scales containing a white powder residue. Eight grams of crack cocaine was found on one of the suspects. Bravo alerted on an article in the bushes outside the building. A semiautomatic weapon was located inside a shoe that belonged to one of the suspects. The officers on the scene stated that without Bravo, some of the drugs and the weapon would have most likely been missed and gone back to the streets.

We are truly blessed with a community that is very supportive of our K-9 units. When there is a need, we can supply it without worrying about budget constraints. We needed life vests for the dogs. I only had to make the need known, and the cost was taken care of by our community. I am very proud of our K-9 teams and what our service means to our community. I feel we really do make a difference. Every time I report for duty, I really do not know what lies around the corner, so I never take anything for granted, nor can I ever become complacent in our attitude or our routine. My aim is to do the very best that Bravo and I can while on duty and to stay safe, so we can go home to our loved ones at the end of our shift.

Officer Joe Veto

Solon Police Department, Solon, Ohio
K-9 REX

Joe just seems so comfortable in his work as a K-9 handler, enjoying his dream job. He has a quiet sense of humor. Rex is a muscle-bound Malinois. Rex came to me and seemed to like being petted. When Joe told me how Rex watched his hands for commands, I watched too. I realized that this gentle dog snuggled against me was the same dog that could cause fear and terror in a bad guy trying to hurt Joe.

I began handling police dogs in the U.S. Air Force in Europe, where I was stationed for four years. I worked with K-9s as a supervisor, trainer, and handler. My air force career started right out of boot camp in Lackland Air Force Base in Texas. After six months of boot camp and military training, I was assigned to a military regiment that provided security to the aircraft and law enforcement for the whole base. One of the police divisions in security was K-9 security and patrol. I made it my passion to become a K-9 handler. You had to be chosen, so the likelihood of becoming one was very remote. One of the new handlers had a dog named Rex. The handler got into trouble, so Rex was given to me as a trained dog. I still needed to be trained, so really Rex was teaching me and leading me. We worked the flight lines behind the airports, guarding the planes against any type of terrorism. Back then we did have terrorism, but no one talked about it. Saboteurs would try to damage our planes. It is the policy for the U.S. Air Force to have security, especially overseas. We had ammo dumps, bunkers, and storage sites. We had nuclear weapons and weapon sites. We used K-9s to patrol the area. We were looking for anyone trying to enter over or under fences. The dogs would alert on movement anywhere in the area that we were protecting. They actually worked the wind. The dogs can scent over a thousand times better than we can. We were sentries; I guess you could call us the warning system. Long ago, bells and tin cans were tied to wire fences. If you heard them rattling at night, you would know someone was coming over the fence. Now we are the rattle.

There were forty-five of us at Lyon, just north of Paris. Later General Charles de Gaulle kicked the United States out of France. I was reassigned to an air force base in Ramstein, Germany. Here our K-9s were trained for aggression, to actually go after a person and hold them. We would follow the leash to the teeth because they would bite and not let go. We had to choke them out. Very seldom could we recall our dogs. We did not train them for recall, as it was not our primary objective. I had the assignment to train dogs for Vietnam. We would go to Cambodia with dogs from Germany and train the forces to utilize the dogs in the proper way. We would leave and repeat the same process. Most of my time was working with my own K-9, Rex.

I had some great experiences in the air force with dogs. It was a very dangerous situation. During the Vietnam era, there were a lot of people who hated us. I was new to the German territory. One day, we had someone trying to sabotage one of our ammo areas. K-9 Rex started chasing him. It was so very cold that night, sub-zero in the mountains. I was wearing a big parka, and I had my hands in the top chest pockets with Rex's leash around my wrist. We were running through the weeds and up and down hills when suddenly Rex led me right over a cliff. My hands were stuck in the pockets. I hit a tree stump at the bottom and was knocked out. The leash was still around my wrist. Rex began dragging me around in the snow.

It took a couple of hours before I was found. The rescue team looked around and saw body tracks where I had been dragged all over the place. Now the problem was for the rescue teams to help me. The K-9 is trained to protect his partner and will often not let anyone get near to help. Sometimes a dog has to be killed in order for a rescue to begin. They really wanted to save him, so they tried to trap and cage him but were unsuccessful. Rex finally allowed the rescue team to help me. The kennel master for the air force kennels who regularly fed Rex was able to secure him and take him back to the kennels. Looking back, I think the fall also had Rex in shock. He was tired from the long, cold tracking and then dragging me around for a few hours. My face was all raw; my eye was hanging out and had to be sewn into the socket. I woke up to see bright lights with doctors talking in German. When I saw the bright lights, I wondered if this was the light I was supposed to see when I died. It was a long four-month recovery, but I made it back to the flight lines with Rex to finish my tour. When my tour was over, I had a very emotional time. I would have to leave Rex. I had a deep love for him. I requisitioned the air force to take Rex home with me. They refused and stated the air force policy of liability: No K-9 would be allowed to leave the service.

It was a very sad day on the kennel floor that day. I sat with Rex and told him I would miss him. He licked my face, and his fur was warm to my face. We sat together, and I thought of the great times we had together, four years of being partners. The U.S. Air Force later had to put Rex down because he refused to be another handler's partner. He was stubborn, just like his partner who was leaving him.

I started in the city of Cleveland as a police officer. I wanted to go into K-9 right after military service. I worked the city streets and worked my way up to being a detective, where I was placed into special assignments. I was assigned to the first sex crimes unit, and then became the police chief's bodyguard. I took one test for the city of Solon at forty-seven years old and was hired. I was the experienced older candidate to add to their young department. Now I had to compete with the younger guys. Being a K-9 handler was my ultimate goal. My chief, Wayne Godzic, was a former handler, so he knew what commitment it took to be a K-9 handler. I was chosen to be the first handler in Solon. My dog was Rex; it seemed ironic that out of all the dogs we could have chosen we chose Rex, with the same name as my dog in the air force. -

K-9 Rex was sworn in as a police office and as my partner. He was born in Amsterdam, Holland, in 2002. He weighs seventy pounds and is certified in the state of Ohio as a dual purpose K-9, drugs and patrol. That means he can do just about anything in drug work. He was taught to alert to drug odor in a passive way, stare, and point to the source. He can track and find suspects as well as lost children or adults. He is also a great partner in protecting me. When given a command, he will bite and apprehend. I can give him verbal commands or hand gestures. He always watches my hands. I have problems with Rex when I give talks to children or adults because I use my hands when I speak for show and to make a point. Rex often keys on my hand gestures, so my audience will begin to laugh as he circles me or disobeys the verbal command.

Rex is very social except when my wife wants to hug and kiss me. He does not like that. He will bark and growl at her. That is a well-told tale throughout the K-9 community—the K-9 being jealous of the affection between the officer and his wife or children.

A lot of police officers think they would like to be a handler, not realizing how much work is involved. They want it because it is different, something new. They don't expect the long hours of training, caring, grooming, and feeding. An officer often spends more time with his K-9 partner than with his wife.

Rex had to have a great drive to be a good drug dog. I have been an officer for thirty years, so nothing surprises me. Drugs are hidden in water, in toilets, and behind walls. The dog is really an asset when the suspect has been sitting in the passenger seat. When Rex alerts at the seat, I know the person sitting there may have drugs hidden on them.

Searching vehicles with a drug dog is quite interesting; the dogs continue to amaze us with their finds. When I am checking a car for drugs, I check three places: the driver's door handle, gas cap, and trunk. If I doubt my K-9 partner, he gets very frustrated with me and grabs at the place and won't let go. I don't want him to be aggressive like that. Once we were searching a car which we knew had drugs. I tried to move Rex away from the back quarter panel. He did not like that. He grabbed the rusted panel in his teeth. He does get upset when I have not trusted him. On training days, I sometimes miss the drugs hidden high up, because his alert is just a snap of his head. I have to watch him as soon as we walk into one of the training rooms to see that quick alert.

I respect animals, but they do not think and process as we do. The instinct of the canine world is the prey drive and survival drive. I can get down on the floor on top of Rex, and he will growl at me. He is a street dog and does not want anyone on top of him, even me! You must show your K-9 partner that you are the alpha dog. He has to see me eat first. I did not play that game in the beginning, and he took advantage of that. He actually sent me to the hospital after he had bitten through my hand. Every time I gave him a command he did not like, he would bite me. After the fourth bite, I was tired of that. Things had to change—and they did. He now bathrooms on command. He doesn't do anything without a command. I also taught my wife how to train him.

People have been very good to me; I have been able to purchase the best equipment. I use a strobe light when tracking at night, so I can see Rex in the distance. When a bad guy is hiding and sees the strobe light on Rex, he gets frightened. The more fear the suspect has, the more odors he gives off. That makes it easy for Rex to sniff and find him. Of all the many dogs I have trained or owned, Rex is by far the very best.

If city hall or the department needs me for an assignment or for public relations, my hours will change. I am on call twenty-four hours a day when needed. If a call comes, I jump out of bed and Rex is already at the door.

I love showing Rex to children. They send posters and letters to me that I treasure. I just tag along at the end of the leash, and Rex steals the show. One of the cutest little girls saw me getting out of my car in town. She turned around and said to her dad, "There's Rex!" The dad asked her if she knew me. She kept saying, "He was at my school." The dad asked if she meant me. She told him, "I never saw him before in my life!" So now I always introduce myself as Officer Joe. I ask the children what my name is; sometimes they remember, and sometimes they don't.

K-9 teams in America are the working force that provides the police department with an additional tool to do their job more efficiently. The canine team searches out drugs, tracks for suspects or lost children, locates evidence, searches buildings, and apprehends criminals. Children relate to the dogs, and they want to know all about them. Their questions lead to a better understanding of why police officers have a K-9, and what kind of help the dogs can really provide to the community. The best feeling of all is when a little boy or girl pets Rex, and he gently kisses them and they squeal or laugh. I know they will be telling their family and friends that they met a real neat police dog and his name is Rex. . . . . By the way, I am Officer Joe.

Officer Jack Waters

Washington, D.C., Police Department, Retired
K-9 MAJOR

For several years, I tried to find a long-retired K-9 handler. I knew the earlier trained dogs were not taught to alert on drugs or explosives, but what did they do? This soft-spoken officer told me about walking a beat with his dog and the pride he had in what they had done as a team.

When I became an officer in the late 1950s, I was issued a gun and a nightstick. I had to buy my flashlight and handcuffs. We wore long-sleeve shirts and ties, and always wore a hat. I walked a beat. I still think that is the best way to know people. I could hear a cry for help. I made many friends along my beat. They would come to my aid when necessary. We did not have radios. If I arrested a suspect, I might have to walk him four or five blocks to a call box for someone to come get my prisoner.

We were some of the first K-9 handlers in the United States. I got Major, a magnificent shepherd. He had a very even disposition. He was strong and very athletic, partly because of the many hours walking my beat. I worked with him even on my days off. When our K-9 unit was formed around 1958 or 1959, we did not have a vehicle to patrol in or to get to our beats, which were all in high-crime areas. We used our own cars and would put the dogs in the back. We bought our own converters and hooked them up to the regular AM/FM radio; this converted our personal car to the police frequency, so we could hear what was going on. We could then respond. This proved very successful. Later we were given a big black car from the White House garage when they replaced one of theirs. It was our first official vehicle, *Cruiser 95*. Two men and two dogs were usually assigned to it, and they had the run of the whole city.

Sometimes we would dress up in old clothes and sit in the parks. We would put our dogs back in the bushes and wait for someone to come rob us. What a surprise they had. Usually, two or three officers would stake out a park. We made lots of cases this way.

We only worked high-crime areas and high-crime hours. A lot of 6 p.m. to 2 a.m., or 7 p.m. to 3 a.m. If I made an arrest, I would have to appear in court at 9 a.m. the next morning, shaved and in a clean uniform. Sometimes I did not get out of court until 3 p.m. and still had to be back on my beat that evening. They wonder why some policemen die so early.

Our dogs were calm on the beat, but in training they would be very aggressive. One time, I had my arm wrapped, but the dog attacked under the wrap. I got bitten and had fourteen stitches and several days off duty. Later I became an assistant trainer.

Eventually in D.C., we got two regular police marked cars and had cages installed in the back for the dogs. One of our training sites was by a barn and huge silo. One of the officers would wrap his arm and pop out from behind the silo and take off running. I would command Major, GET 'EM! One time, to see what would happen, twenty officers popped out from behind the silo. My dog was commanded, GET 'EM! But on seeing twenty officers, he seemed dumbfounded and simply stood still.

I walked beats in high-crime areas. I have been shot at and threatened with knives. That is all part of being an officer walking a beat. I went where the crime was, and it was no picnic. Our dogs were great trackers; often they could follow a track three or four days old.

A man, his wife, and his daughter were visiting from Georgia. They left their car unlocked while they visited the Botanic Garden. The lady got anxious and sent her husband back to the car to retrieve her purse and the daughter's camera. When the man got to his car, he saw two teenagers inside. They fled the scene. There weren't any Park Police available, so I was called to track the fleeing teens. I put Major's tracking harness on him, and we began to track through the woods to a river. Several people were fishing. I asked if they had seen two boys run past them. From the looks on their faces, I believe they had seen the boys, but they said they had not seen them. I was discouraged. Fifty yards later, Major stopped. I looked at the river and saw a lady's purse floating on top of the water. I took his tracking harness off and told him FETCH. He brought the purse back to me. I put his tracking harness on again. He led me to some small trees with many leaves on the ground. He again alerted. I said, FIND

AND FETCH. He began to dig in the leaves and found the lady's coat. That vacationing family was very happy. When they returned to Georgia, they sent a letter to the Chief of Police. I was given a commendation!

One day I was patrolling the northeast section of Washington, D.C., in one of our marked K-9 cars. It was a very hot July day, not much was going on. I had parked by the Anacostia River, so Major could have a little swim to cool off. He loved that. A pickup truck pulled up along side of my cruiser. The driver told me that there was a car in the middle of Pennsylvania and Fairlawn Avenues with a big woman pulling up her dress and flashing everyone. He told me I must go see that because it was so funny. He said it looked like the "Orange Moon Over Miami." He said I would die laughing. I got Major back into the cruiser and went to find the car.

Traffic was functioning well. No moon shining. The driver of the pickup had given me the license number and make of the car. Fifty yards down the street, I found it. I left Major in my car. I could see a figure with a wig on sideways, the hair was hanging down in his face, and he even had a dress on. I asked him what he was doing. He stuttered and stammered. I asked to see his driver's license and registration. The car engine was running, and the window was down. As he was reaching for the registration, I reached inside to grab the keys to turn off the engine. That sucker put the window up on my right arm and stepped on the gas, and down Fairlawn Avenue we went. I grabbed the steering wheel with my right hand and the rain gutter with my left hand. The car gradually came across the road and hit the bank on the other side. We had gone almost hundred feet down the road at about 45 mph. I could hear Major barking back in my car where I left him. When the car hit the bank, my arm broke the window. Somehow I got into the car and kicked the guy out the other side. I smacked him with my blackjack, and then handcuffed him to the door handle. I walked back to my cruiser to call for transport. The only reason I did not shoot him was my gun was on the same side as my arm in the window. He was placed under arrest and the moon shone no more.

After twenty years with the police department, I do have a few stories to tell. I made many good friends. I really liked my job. I have a lot of good memories.

Master Officer Todd Van Dresar

College Station Police Department, College Station, Texas

K-9 BRANDO

I have not met Todd in person. I was checking the Amazon.com rating for my children's book and found his review. He gave my book a five-star rating and wrote: "A Great Read! This book has given my daughter an understanding of the job I do as a K-9 handler in a way that makes reading fun for her." Now what writer could resist such a flattering review? I was able to contact him, and here is his story of finding his first bomb.

Imagine a U.S. Marine, in the middle of a hostile neighborhood in the Middle East, standing over a wounded marine, fighting off an unknown number of assailants until help arrives. When all is said and done, that marine will probably get a medal for his actions, possibly even the Congressional Medal of Honor. The newspapers will ask for an interview; the soldier's family will be on TV telling the country how proud they are of their child. That same marine would be asked to speak at college graduations, and military schools, and will meet the president.

Unfortunately, most officers in this country and the people we protect aren't aware that K-9 partners show that same bravery every day. No pay raises, no speaking engagements, and no presidential kudos for this hero—just some playtime with his handler and his favorite toy. It takes a special type of dog and a special type of police officer to form a K-9 team.

When I was finishing my initial training with a patrol explosives-detection partner, a call came from the sheriff's office of a nearby county. They were serving a search warrant on the home of an extremist militant, who was rumored to be stockpiling explosives on his property. They wanted our assistance. After getting the go-ahead, we drove to the house located in a rural area. While on the way, all I could think about was, *This is what we've working for all these months. It is game time. Don't blow up!*

When we got there, we met with the deputies and agents handling the investigation. They let us know that this guy had been overheard telling people that he had booby-trapped his home specifically for law enforcement. *Great!* I am thinking. *This gets better and better.* I was comforted a little when I learned that our bomb techs had already checked out the place for traps. But it's always in the back of the mind of an explosives dog handler that there could be more traps. My trainer was my backup officer. He and I donned SWAT gear. We did a preliminary check of the house and layout. Looking at the inside of this place, there were literally piles and piles of ammo crates, clothes, and boxes filling the house. There were paths weaving around, a million places to hide his stuff, and a million places to booby-trap. I got my K-9 partner out of the car, and we started doing our thing. It was as though he knew it was for real. He was stepping over things on the floor and moving around objects without bumping into them. This helped me greatly considering I had a Kevlar helmet on (something I hadn't trained with) that kept dropping to cover my eyes. As we were moving through the house, Brando sniffed a trash can that was near a wall. He paused and sniffed again and then sat with a perfect "vulture stare." My partner and I just looked at each other with that *uh-oh* expression on our faces and moved him down the wall. I wanted to be sure, so I worked him down the same wall after searching the bedroom. Same trash can, same result. Now the "pucker factor" is in full effect. The can is full of paper towels, and I cannot see the bottom. For two months, Brando has been finding explosive odors in places I never thought possible. We only use real explosives to train with, not pseudo. So I *know* my dog has caught wind of something real. This guy probably knew we would be looking through his trash for evidence. I thought this could be a trap.

We backed out and let the explosive techs know what we had found. I felt so proud watching them going into the house with full gear to check it out. A few minutes later, they came back out with one of those set-and-leave bug spray cans. Yes, a BUG BOMB. I knew it was not the can Brando hit on, but probably one of the towels that the suspect used after handling his stash. I still got ribbed about Brando finding his first "bomb." It was all in good fun, though. I think the joking was more or less letting out the tension of the whole event and the danger we all faced that night, including Brando—who was closer to the danger than any of us. I later learned that several hand grenades were found as well as an automatic weapon in a different place on the same property.

Officer Jimmie Davenport

Austin Police Department, Austin, Texas

K-9s AMMO AND STUKA

Officer Davenport tells stories when he is giving his presentations to the Citizen Police Academy. He said it helps illustrate that police officers, especially K-9 handlers, have a unique perspective on police work and animals, as well as a sense of humor.

The persistent beeping from my pager brings my evening off to an abrupt end. I'm a K-9 officer on callback for SWAT missions. I gather my gear like a fighter pilot hearing the alert and fly out the door with my K-9 Ammo. A police call in Austin, Texas, has just become a SWAT call-up.

Using police service dogs in SWAT operations is a relatively new concept. A police dog trained in the SWAT arena is a valuable tool and asset. These dogs require specialized training, as do their handlers. They must become a smooth, seamless member of the team. This requires hours of extra training, and the K-9 itself must be an exceptional animal. The training consists of working with and in gas environments, all the while understanding the commands of their handler through a gas mask. The dogs are exposed to weapons that are fired over, next to, and in very close proximity to their heads. They work very close to men in heavy combat vests that resemble bite suits, and they have to be very quiet and patient for hours on end. To be called a SWAT dog is a hard-earned honor from the SWAT team members.

When I arrive at the apartment complex where the call originated, I see the usual stirred anthill of activity associated with a SWAT call-up. SWAT officers getting prepared for the call look like bulging green beetles with their helmets, weapons, and large combat vests full of specialized equipment. Uniformed police officers are in various conversations with people displaced from their apartments who are just trying to get a sliver more of information. An EMS truck sits idling with the crew on standby, hoping they are not called to the scene. Command personnel speak into their headsets glancing at charts, and cast concerned looks as information begins coming in from the various intelligence officers who are poring over police data extracted from various sources. It's never lost on me how one person's actions can affect so many others' lives.

I begin to transform myself from the *Monday Night Football* junkie I was thirty minutes ago to assuming that beetle look myself. On goes my combat vest weighing over thirty pounds. It's packed with rations, dog food, rifle magazines, spare pistol magazines, gas mask, water for the dog, spare flashlights, batteries, thirty-foot leash, wire cutters, binoculars, medical supplies, and host of other K-9 needs and personal gear. Kneepads, helmet, balaclava, and radio headset complete the transformation. I strap my K-9 into his harness and electronic collar. We are fit for duty and ready to immerse ourselves into the call-up.

I report into the command post and receive my briefing from the on-scene commander. A man who is determined to be emotionally disturbed has barricaded himself in his second-story apartment. There are indications he may have a nine-year-old child in the apartment and the child may be a potential hostage. The suspect was making threatening remarks to the officers stationed on the perimeter and started tossing household items out the second-story window.

I was attached to a three-man element, and our task was to maintain a containment perimeter on the apartment front door. We were not to allow the suspect past us and be prepared to make a move if the child could be rescued. The element leader and I formed a game plan of "if this, then we do that." SWAT operations are never cut-and-dried affairs, there is always something changing in the dynamics, despite what Hollywood would lead you to believe.

In my headset, I hear a team leader expressing a concern to the command post that he is afraid the suspect may leap out the second-story window and flee in the courtyard below, which has multiple escape points. The team leader wants to redeploy me and my K-9 to the overhang, which is adjacent to the open window below, but out of sight of the suspect. He receives an approval to redeploy us, and we make our way to the new position. Once again, I discuss all possibilities of action with my new element leader. Satisfied we've thought of all contingencies, we settle in for what looks to be another long night's wait.

My headset continues to provide dialogue between the command elements. A hostage negotiator attempts in vain to get the suspect on the telephone to talk over the situation. Snipers are giving periodic updates on the suspect. Team leaders are refining options. Personnel are shuffled to more advantageous positions. More intelligence comes in that maybe the nine-year-old isn't in the apartment or a hostage. At this point, the suspect becomes quite agitated. He throws more household debris out his window, and it crashes into the concrete sidewalk. I'm trying to figure out what the debris is and wonder why people destroy their own property at times like this. My K-9 hears the man's yelling and looks to me for guidance. He knows something is happening, and we've seen this behavior before from suspects. His anticipation is growing, as is mine.

We hear from the upstairs window shouts of "I have a knife" and another muffled comment about having an "a nine-millimeter pistol with one bullet." I'm running my hand down Ammo's back. Now all the training for hours pays off. He is ready to go at a word's notice but knows I require absolute calm from him despite the rising tension. I smell smoke. When a house burns, it smells a certain way. My element members and I look at one another. We are silently asking one another, "Do you smell what I smell?" I see smoke coming from the upstairs window of the suspect's window. My headset comes to life with radio transmissions of orders and contingency plans. Snipers are verifying smoke is coming from the suspect's window. I think to myself that this is getting really interesting.

Plans to deploy tear gas are quickly made. We are going to force the suspect from his apartment. We cannot allow a fire to get out of control in the apartment complex. My element and I pull our gas masks from our combat vests and in well-rehearsed fashion strip off our helmets and place them over our faces. The straps fall into place and are pulled on with a sense of urgency. This time it's real, not a training exercise. I smell the familiar rubbery odor of the mask. I seal it to my face with both hands over the exhaust ports and am satisfied I am prepared to make entry into that apartment if called upon. I strap my helmet back on and readjust all my gear accordingly.

The team leader preps two gas grenades. He quickly goes over his deployment routine with us. We know who is going to cover him; we know which way he will move and how we will move when he's done throwing the grenades into the apartment windows. One final radio call to the command post and the go-ahead to deploy gas is given. I watch the team leader pull one pin from a grenade, and he gives it a heave into the window. He quickly pulls the second pin and places the second grenade perfectly into the same window. I can't help but watch as a spectator would at a sporting contest. I am sometimes in awe that I am paid to do this for a living.

Just after the second gas grenade spins end over end into the apartment window, the suspect vaults out from the second-story window and crashes headfirst into the grass at our feet. He is merely eight feet from us. Like a scene from a cheap slasher movie, I can see that the man has attempted to cut his own throat on both sides. He does not have a shirt on. His chest is covered in fresh blood. Two huge gory holes in his neck glare angrily back at us from the harsh white light from a SWAT officer's carbine. The man has a huge butcher knife in his right hand. He looks right at us, and I've seen those eyes before. Those are the eyes not of a human but that of a trapped animal. Wild. Predatory.

The SWAT officer with the less lethal shotgun—which fires bean-bag munitions intended to stun a person and not kill them—skillfully places two shots on the man's torso. The shots knock the butcher knife from the man's grasp, but he does not surrender. The team leader is giving firm commands for the man to lie down and place his hands behind his back. He hesitates, but begins to do as he is told. I think this will end in moments. I glance up at the window where the man came from. Orange flames can be seen inside the apartment. Thick smoke is now billowing from the window. It is a gray-and-white concoction of CS gas and burning apartment. My eyes come back to the suspect, who I expect to see fully prepared to surrender and be handcuffed. He begins to get unruly and uncooperative. The team leader senses we are losing the element of command and dominance. The team leader fires a Taser, which injects two probes into a person, and they carry an electric current designed to overwhelm the motor senses and render a person unable to fight or flee. But both probes must inject themselves into the person to close the electrical circuit and render it ineffective. I see one probe is, in fact, in the man and the other burrowed into the dirt. The Taser won't work. Reloading a new Taser cartridge will take a few seconds.

With no warning and in a blink of the eye, the suspect has gone from the facedown position to running away from us. In my sixteen years of police work, I've never seen a man move that fast from that position to a dead sprint. This guy is fast! The less lethal SWAT officer continues firing beanbags, but they miss. The team leader instinctively runs after the suspect. We know this man may be armed with that 9 mm pistol. He's running toward a breezeway where the apartment's residents are lined up outside the yellow crime scene tape. I can see the residents from my position.

My element leader is yelling "Dog!" Time stands still. I release my gloved grip on Ammo's harness, and he is instantly at full speed. I'm watching a fighter plane zero in on its opponent blindside. He tracks and mimics the suspect's movement like a missile with one purpose. In a blur, he jets by the team leader who seems to be running in quicksand compared to the speed displayed by my Malinois. I'm also running but don't remember doing so. I see Ammo's sledgehammer blow arrive in the man's buttocks. The impact drives the suspect into the parking lot face-first. Ammo does as he is trained to do: Hold the suspect until I tell him to release the man. The suspect continues to resist. He is striking Ammo about his body with his fists, but Ammo is not deterred. We've trained for this. He is a warrior. I command Ammo to release the suspect, and he complies. He returns to me, and we prepare for what may happen next. The team leader fires the Taser with proper results this time. The suspect surrenders. The fire is extinguished. There wasn't a nine-year-old hostage. The man wasn't armed. The man was emotionally disturbed and had a crack cocaine problem. Thankfully, no one was else was injured.

Later, as I drive to the hospital to check on the suspect's medical status, I'm struck by the professionalism of the SWAT officers I serve with, and am glad we train to the standards that we do. As I continue to drive on the freeway, I smile a big toothy smile. I'm proud of Ammo because he ended a potentially deadly situation and all he wanted was a pat on the head for his efforts. I turn on my good times radio to ESPN Sports and wonder who won the *Monday Night Football* game.

In 1997, about 2 a.m., a patrol shift requested a K-9 search of a mortuary. There had been a rash of mortuary burglaries for the embalming fluid. It was used to dip marijuana cigarettes into, to increase the high received. When I arrived with my K-9 partner Stuka, I saw the open back door bathed in police spotlights and intense reflections from the high beams of the angled patrol cars illuminating the back wall.

As soon as I stepped out of my patrol car, I had a chill go down my spine. A mortuary contains dead people. Frankenstein and Dracula and the Mummy were in my mind. Before I can explain what occurred inside the building, one must understand my upbringing as a young boy in the 1970s. I was the kid who on Friday night watched *Creature Feature,* which came on at 10 p.m. It hosted the monster movies of that era. I would settle down on the couch with a Jiffy Pop bag of popcorn fresh off the stove, the large aluminum dome steaming with buttery smells. I had my trusty Coke to wash it down as the movie would begin. I saw them all: *Frankenstein, Dracula, The Wolfman, The Mummy,* and every Peter Cushing movie in between. I was a monster movie junkie.

Fast-forward to my police call for a K-9 search of such a place where I had seen untold horror in my childhood caused me to pause for a second. But I am a grown man in my thirties with a police dog. I had to giggle to myself. There aren't really monsters in mortuaries. Right?

I was briefed by on-the-scene officers. It was a door alarm, not a motion alarm, where something was moving inside the building. A worker may have left the door ajar, and the wind blew it open. Just like in the movies.

I had given my verbal warning for the phantom suspect to come out or a police dog was coming in. After the required waiting period, I commanded Stuka to begin our search. As I stepped inside, all the lights were out. The building was huge, nearly a city block long. I knew I would be in there for quite some time. For some reason, I began to hear that creepy organ music in my head. That slow building in tone, signaling to movie-watchers that a character is getting close to something they don't want to see. I advanced through the building, using my flashlight only to illuminate the searched areas. I saw shadow shapes on the wall look like arms moving, and that creepy music kept building in my head.

I moved through the viewing rooms where the thick scent of fresh flowers still hung in the air. My mind said, *A dead person was in here today.* The only thing missing was a flash of lightning and the crash of thunder.

The search was coming to an end, and I knew I had covered the city block by my experience in doing hundreds of building searches. Up to this point, Stuka had not given me any indication of a human presence.

I came to the long, narrow hallway that turned to the left. I fed out Stuka on his leash to make the turn and clear the immediate area. He went around the corner, went two feet, and stopped. I use a ten-foot leash, so I knew he still had plenty more room to go. Why did he stop? Is there a door around the corner? Is this a building exit? I cautiously leaned around the corner allowing my flashlight to briefly light up the side hallway. I saw my dog had stopped in the middle of the hallway, his ears were up and his head cocked to the right. I looked past him to see what looked like a person looking at me. The person appeared to be lying on his side partially wrapped in a sheet. But he wasn't moving. I stepped back behind the corner. Did I just see a person looking at me? Why is he lying on his side? Is that a dead person? Why is that organ music suddenly louder?

I peered back around the corner to confirm what I had seen. I leaned further out into the hallway to get a better look at the person. What I had not seen was a coat tree, which was painted white and matched the color of the wall. It was a detail I had missed. As I leaned out in the hallway, my right shoulder suddenly felt a *tap-tap-tap* as if someone was trying to get my attention. I knew full well no one was with me. Stuka was here, and the backup officers were only a room away. *No one should be there.* I knew Frankenstein had me! I looked at my right shoulder where the tapping was coming from. I saw an apparition of a white lab coat shake side-to-side only inches from me. In the dimly lit hallway with me seeing monsters in every room, it seemed to be a ghost after me.

I screamed and attacked the lab coat; I grabbed it and wanted to go out with a fight. I fought the lab coat to the floor, and my K-9 came to my rescue. Stuka grabbed the evil lab coat, and I was trying to figure out why the coat had stopped attacking me. Meanwhile my backup officers were rushing to my aid, guns drawn ready for anything. I sheepishly saw that a haunted lab coat had attacked me.

Yes, there was a body in the preparation room. I never went in there. I had the backup officers check that. For years onward, I was always reminded by those officers about the attack of the lab coat.

Cadaver Searches

Trooper Matt Zarrella

Rhode Island State Police, Scituate, Rhode Island
with **John Turco**, DVM, Rhode Island State Police Veterinarian
K-9s HANNIBAL, GUNNER, PANZER, AND MAXIMUS

This is a rare story of a patriotic adventure by two non-military
men who were willing to take great risks to honor a request from
their government.

I do not consider myself an expert but I have been handling police dogs
trained in the location of human remains for the Rhode Island State
Police for fifteen of my sixteen-year career. Hannibal, a Greater Swiss
mountain dog, was my first trained cadaver dog for the Rhode Island
State Police. He was not picked for the specific task of being a search-
and-rescue dog. Hannibal was my companion dog before I became a state
trooper and was later trained in search and rescue. He was a very large
dog, weighing in at approximately 130 pounds. But he was very loving
and gentle. However, he was a slow worker who was motivated by food.
Connecticut State Trooper Andrew Redman trained Hannibal and me.
Andy was not a big fan of Greater Swiss mountain dogs, but agreed to
train us privately. His outlook on our situation was that he would get
Hannibal and me to a point where we were operational and later find me
a highly motivated German shepherd to work.

To my surprise, Hannibal rose to the occasion on each and every
search and became probably the most well-known search-and-rescue dog
in Rhode Island. He died suddenly and unexpectedly from bloat in 1996
at the age of six, but not before leaving an impressive record of public
service. Between 1992 and 1996, he was credited with finding ten bodies
and two live persons. He had worked on over a hundred searches, many
of them speculative with no definite information. This record included a
mission with the FBI in a search of a mass grave in Cali, Colombia, South
America, in connection with that country's war with drug cartels.

During the summer of 1993, I was at the memorial service for a

Westerly police officer's dog that had been killed by a passing car while the two were jogging on a secondary road. At the end of the service a man and woman approached the officer, me, and a few other police officers. They were holding an eight-week-old German shepherd puppy in their arms. They asked the Westerly officer if he wanted the puppy. We were all stunned by the offer, but the officer declined because he already had another dog coming as a replacement. The couple seemed confused and said they had brought the puppy to donate to him. Then they asked if any of us wanted her. They told us they would only donate her to a police officer who wanted a working dog. Everyone looked at me because they knew that Hannibal and I had been very busy over the last year and that we could have used some help. I accepted and took the female puppy home. I named her Panzer. When she was a year old, we had already begun her specialty scent work. To date, Panzer is the longest-working dog I have owned and the most successful in finding missing persons as well as finding buried bodies.

Panzer also went to South America with me and worked long enough to travel to Southeast Asia with me in 2003, where we were assigned to the U.S. military for a special mission. We were to assist in locating the remains of missing servicemen from the Vietnam War. Dogs can be trained to smell human remains including blood, bones, and teeth that are even underwater or have been buried for a number of years, or soil that has been around a cadaver. I have had dogs alert on graves as far back as the 1930s. Panzer had a long and distinguished career with the Rhode Island State Police. She worked on over three hundred cases and located many live persons as well as deceased subjects. At the invitation of a combination of local, state, and federal authorities, Panzer and I traveled over much of the Northeast assisting on missing person cases.

In January 2000, we were asked to assist in an ongoing search for the remains of a six-year-old girl. We had been assisting investigators on and off since 1995, searching various locations in and around Massachusetts and Rhode Island. These areas were specifically related to where the suspect had previously resided and areas he frequented. However, in January 2000, new information lead us to Bethesda, Maryland, where we were asked by the Montgomery County Police and the FBI to conduct a search in an area down an embankment along a highway approximately three acres in size. The search took us two days, but on the second day, Panzer gave a very convincing alert coming within a few feet of the grave. The suspect said he had left a two-foot by two-foot piece of box spring on top of the grave to mark it.

After a brief search in the immediate area, Detective Ed Taney of the Montgomery Police Department located a small piece of wire sticking out of the ground several feet from Panzer's alert. The wire was what was left of the marker left by the suspect to mark the grave sixteen years earlier. At that moment, I could not have been any prouder of Panzer. She went on to work many more cases and she had many finds. She died at age eleven after a brief battle with cancer.

In 1996, Norm and Delano Christensen, who believed in using these dogs for search and rescue, donated another Greater Swiss mountain dog named Gunner to me. Gunner worked with me for six years. The FBI asked me to assist investigators in the search of a body of a homicide suspect missing six years. The information cultivated by investigators led them to the backyard of a residence owned by the assailant. The yard had been previously dug up with a backhoe, and there were deep holes all around the yard. As I was working Gunner around the property, we came to a cement slab that I quickly worked him around. The slab was approximately ten feet by ten feet and approximately four inches thick.

As Gunner worked one side of the slab, I observed a very weak change in body language accompanied by strong eye contact. I noted this and continued working him in other areas to see if the scent was coming from somewhere else. I redirected him over the cement slab a second time, then a third, each time taking him out to work in another area. Each time he went over this particular corner of the slab, he reacted the same way he had when he first encountered it.

At the conclusion of the search, I advised the investigators that I thought Gunner had located a very weak scent at the base of the cement slab. They informed me they would look into the area further. At that point, I loaded Gunner into my vehicle and returned to Rhode Island.

I would later learn that they took up the cement slab and dug a hole nine feet deep and located the body. It had been wrapped tightly in plastic, then a tarp and then a rug and buried under some wood. Even after six years in the ground, the body was so well preserved that the police were able to identify some tattoos that assisted them in the identification.

I had been talking with representatives from the U.S. military about a possible mission to Vietnam, with the tentative date set for February 2003. It was now the end of June 2002. If I was going to conduct this mission, I knew I needed another dog fast. The dog not only had to be found but had to be socialized, trained in cadaver search, and certified within the given time frame, which only left me about six months to do it.

I scoured the dog pounds and shelters, testing dogs to see if I could find the right dog at the right age. I wanted to get a German shepherd, and I wanted it to be a rescue dog, because I believe in giving an unwanted dog a chance to be helped and to go on to help others.

Shortly thereafter, my prayers were answered when a friend informed me of a six-month-old German shepherd puppy at the local pound. This puppy apparently was too aggressive and had been turned in by a family with small children. He had been at the shelter for two weeks, and no one had showed any interest in him.

A good friend of mine, a patrol dog trainer for the Rhode Island State Police, and I drove to the shelter the next day to look at the dog. I knew immediately that he was the one. As for aggressiveness, well, he just had a whole lot of energy and nowhere to release it.

I took him home and named him Maximus, after the Roman general. We immediately started training from basic obedience to specialty scent work. I knew that Maximus had to come around and learn everything needed to locate buried bodies in an almost unheard-of time frame. If this plan worked, Maximus would be fully trained and certified as a cadaver dog when he was eleven months old. In January, he finished his training and was certified. Mr. Rebmann flew in from Washington State to conduct the test, which Maximus passed with flying colors. Mr. Rebmann has an international and impeccable reputation for training search-and-rescue dogs. He is also known for administering difficult tests. He had nothing but praise for my dog.

People often ask me how a dog that is trained for cadaver search can distinguish the scent of a dead person from other odors in the environment. We train the dogs to ignore the odors of dead animals and other distractions often found in the environment. They are taught to focus on the odor of human decomposition. It is amazing to watch the dogs do this when properly trained.

The idea for a mission to Vietnam came about when a relative of a missing serviceman was attending a meeting of League of Families in Washington, D.C. In the audience were members of the Joint Task Force for the Full Accounting for the Location and Recovery of Human Remains. Their job was to search for Americans still unaccounted for in Southeast Asia.

A lady asked the officials why dogs had not been used to assist the searches. One high-ranking military official said he did not know why dogs had not been tried and promised to look into the prospect of using them.

John: The military began to look into such a mission. Matt's name kept coming up, as he is an authority on cadaver searching. There are not a lot of people trained to do this. They kept talking to Matt, and finally they asked if he was interested. He said he would go if he could have veterinarian assistance. He asked me if I was interested. Yes! The military approved of me to be part of the team.

Matt: Representatives from the military were very pleased that I was able to bring two cadaver dogs to assist with the mission. I had suggested possibly bringing another dog handler, but was advised that there was not enough room in the helicopters for another person. As I look back on my decision to go to Vietnam at that time, I realize I really gambled on my ability to prepare my dogs and myself.

Shortly after I was asked to assist with the mission, Gunner had been diagnosed with cancer. That was rough for me to take as Gunner was very experienced at cadaver search, and he was my partner and my friend. I still had Panzer, who was my most experienced cadaver dog, but because she was nine years old I could not expect her to carry the whole mission.

I had Maximus, who at the time was just wild, out-of-control six-month-old puppy. I was not sure I would have him trained in time, but I had no choice. I had to. I conducted some form of training every day for the next six months, including Christmas and New Year's Day. I needed every day I had available to me if we were to finish in time.

Once ready to deploy, the team would consist of the following personnel: a captain as team leader, a medic, an information specialist, an anthropologist, an explosive specialist, myself, John Turco, DVM, and K-9s Panzer and Maximus.

News of the mission spread quickly, and *Animal Planet* and *National Geographic* wanted to send representatives to accompany us to Vietnam.

However, the Vietnamese government said no. They disapproved of media coverage filming body recoveries. We traveled to Hawaii to join our team, receive briefings, and undergo some field testing. The army wanted to see the dogs work for themselves.

One of the tests we participated in was a search for two human bones almost fifty years old, recovered from the time of the Korean War. The bones were buried in an area along with a pig bone and a plastic human bone.

The test was for the benefit of the whole team, who accompanied us on the search. The bones were buried several days in advance. On the day of the search, the whole team assembled on the macadam and boarded a Black Hawk helicopter. We were flown to the search area and dropped off. Our explosive specialist conducted a simulated sweep for any ordnance. Our information specialist had to figure out where the actual search area was. We had to hike a short distance to the search area, but once there, we were told there were actually three separate search areas to check. One area actually had nothing buried in it at all. I conducted the searches without prior knowledge of where the items were buried. After checking the first two sites without receiving any alerts, I was confident the last site held the clues. At the third site, I received the alerts I was looking for. The human bones were recovered. The dogs did a great job, and the team was gaining respect for the dogs.

John: We had brainstormed on how we would cool the dogs in the Vietnamese heat. We came up with the idea of using a plant mister filled with cool water. We would mist the dogs, and the evaporation would cool them. We also used wet towels draped over them when they were resting.

Matt: It was oppressively hot in Vietnam. We soon realized that our dogs were working less than 50 percent efficient by midmorning. At times because of the logistics of getting to the actual search site, we had to push the dogs to work until two or three o'clock in the afternoon. Fortunately, John would keep one dog as cool as he could while the other one worked. We alternated them as much as possible. Their actual work time in the field was approximately fifteen minutes at a time. We carried our own backpacks with our own IVs and food for the day. The packs were about fifty pounds each. John's pack was heavier as he had far more gear to carry with the dogs' medical supplies.

While hiking from a search one afternoon, we were climbing up a steep incline with the temperature about 105 degrees. We stopped to rest at least three times before reaching the top. Our dogs were overheated. Our team also needed to rest. At one point during the hike, John and the team medic collapsed under the weight of their packs and needed to be assisted. I helped John carry his pack for a short time.

John: When we looked at the thermometer, we thought it was broken, as it was 105 to 110 degrees. That reading was taken under the tarp with a bit of shade. The dogs were kept on doxycycline to prevent infection from bacteria found in the local water. We were also on the drug to prevent malaria. Matt kept his canteen filled. At any sign of thirst, the dogs were given water. Hydration was so important for both the dogs and us.

Matt: We were to search the sites given to us. If the dogs alerted, we were to dig there. The military did not realize that when a dog alerts on a thirty- or forty-year-old site it does not mean any remains would be right there. The groundwater over the years may take the scent to a different spot. It depends on the pitch of the land and the water table. It becomes an art and a science to conduct a cadaver search.

John: Initially, we were given fifteen to seventeen sites. We only got to eight of them. The dogs alerted to three or four out of the eight. We were given a day or so at each site. In the United States when Matt searches a site, he will go back a number of times to try to hone in on the best place to dig. Our team and the Vietnamese would get together to decide the sites. The officials in each province had to give us permission. Did we have the witnesses lined up? Many days we had plans to go to a certain site, but the official would not appear. The Vietnamese were very friendly, but still we always needed permission. A witness might tell us a body was buried right over there thirty years ago right under that bunch of trees. But our dogs had alerted fifty yards away. Who owns that land? We needed each owner's permission to dig. It became politics. It was very difficult to search in deep jungle if the dogs were on leash. However, I was nervous about snakes. There are many kinds of poisonous snakes in Vietnam, but thank God we had no direct contact. We did see a green viper, which is pretty deadly. Before we went, I thought there would be a snake every five feet in the jungle! We did not take antivenom, as we could not keep it cold. We took our chances. I would have needed fifty vials per dog per bite per snake. I would have needed three hundred to four hundred vials. The military simply put an evacuation plan in place should anything happen. The biggest problems remained the heat, the wild pigs, and the wild dogs. We did carry a dog repellent that is like mace. The Vietnamese had never seen large dogs and were afraid of them.

Matt: We thought we would helicopter to our site and stay in tents. The military wanted to investigate official sites that would require long hikes in and we would stay in tents overnight. The Vietnamese government would not allow that. They did not want to stay overnight in the jungle even though there could be good finds for the Americans. As cases got changed around, we just did the best we could. The Vietnamese officials came dressed in shirts with collars, slacks, and sneakers. They did not have packs or any resources. They did not want to get dirty in a tent. They would get paid the same without staying overnight in the jungle. We were told they were being paid very well. They had to always be with us, so we all stayed in hotels with our dogs.

The witnesses were not always truthful, but the dogs became the truth serum. When they saw the dogs, they would suddenly say, "No body!" Maybe they wanted their fifteen minutes of fame? We were dealing with forty-year-old memories. I thought if a primary witness had actually seen an American body being buried, it would be ingrained in his mind. He might embellish it a bit. But a body buried in the triple canopy jungle where every tree looks the same was so difficult. Was an American seen being buried under that big tree or this one? We were told that if the Vietnamese would come up with American remains they would be paid. They would go out and find remains not American and doctor them to make them look American. But those were not American bones. The information is out there, some of it is good but a lot is not. As information is passed down it is changed. A farmer had told his sons never to plow a certain field because an American was buried there. We searched with the dogs and no alerts. Maybe there was not enough decayed material to scent. We believe no body was buried there.

John: The military were extremely hard workers. They did everything they could for the dogs. If I asked for shade, they would cut bamboo for a lean-to each day. If I needed water, they would find it. If I needed help carrying my pack, they did it. Matt was sick for five days. Three of those days, he was flat in bed. Two of those days, he did manage to go out on the search, and the military carried his pack. After the whole mission was finished, I told Matt I would be willing to give up everything if the military would put together a special team that did only this, searching and finding MIAs. It was such a great experience. I am forty-five years old, and for the first time in my life this just hit me. WOW! Maybe this is the reason I am here.

Matt: The effects of what we have accomplished in Vietnam have yet to be seen. However, I believe the mission is already a success based on what we have already done. We were able to overcome the logistics of never knowing how to pull this mission off. By being selected and actually going in the country and performing the mission with the dogs and without anyone getting hurt was remarkable, because so many people did not think it could be done. Any K-9 that had been used by the military in the Vietnamese War did not come home. Our dogs were the first to go back to Vietnam to participate in something that had to do with that war. We got our dogs into the country and back home alive.

Additionally, the dogs have been credited with alerting to an area and verifying a crash site of an American F-5 Freedom Fighter that was shot down in South Vietnam in 1965. The crash site itself no longer held any remains of the plane, but the anthropologists dug an area approximately ten meters by ten meters and located remnants of the pilot's uniform, life-support system, and personal items he had with him. To me, this was a remarkable find for the dogs, as there were still enough residual odors at the crash site from the now-decomposed remains to alert the dogs.

I feel extremely honored to have been a part of this great and noble mission. The men and women of the U.S. military who do this regularly are remarkable people. I have great respect and admiration for them because it is a dangerous job to volunteer for. I would be willing to do this again if asked and I know Dr. John Turco would, too. Do you know why? Because to have the chance to find one missing American is what it is all about. It is not just about the dogs or the anthropologists, or the military, although they all are an extremely important part. It is about finding and bringing home missing Americans. This is what we all want to do, and that is what I want to do. Perhaps in the future, when I retire from the Rhode Island State Police, I may get another opportunity to go back and do it again.

Captain Sandra Lesko

Firefighter Paramedic, Willoughby Hills Fire Department
Willoughby Hills, Ohio
K-9s GONDO AND ELIOT NESS

Sandy is both a captain with her fire department and a cadaver dog handler with Geauga County Sheriff's Office and the FBI as needed. Sandy is a slim blonde who seems very at ease in two usually male-dominated professions. K-9 Eliot Ness sniffed around my home as Sandy told me about her work with cadaver dogs.

I had been working with dogs in search and rescue before I got Gondo. People from Russell Township had imported him from Denmark. He turned out to be simply too much dog for them. The owners wanted him to go into a working environment. Through friends, I ended up with him. He is a high-drive working dog; once I gave him a job, he was great. He had to have something to do, or he would get bored and be destructive. He could not be just a pet. We started with search and rescue doing tracking and finding live victims. There was not enough work for us. Cadaver work seemed so much more interesting to me. I was interested in the forensics. I had the medical background as a firefighter paramedic for twenty years. Gondo did not love working cadaver, but he liked it and was very good at it. K-9 Eliot loves cadaver work; it is all he knows. I became busy with cadaver work right from the beginning. We did land cadaver searches and water searches looking for drowning victims. I had an average fifteen to twenty call-outs a year.

I was watching the horror unfold on TV on 9/11. When the buildings collapsed, I knew I could help. I had approval through our fire department, and the Geauga County Sheriff's Office supported me also. I went to New York City five days after the attack. I took bottled water and food rations, but found out there were plenty of supplies there. I knew going there what to expect. I did not expect to find live bodies or even whole bodies. I knew we would be finding parts of bodies. I went to work with my dog and to find cadaver parts, so I could help bring closure to the families. I knew it would be a gruesome sight. Gondo is an athlete as I am; we run together almost every day, so he was in good shape. He did wear booties, as there was so much glass and shards of metal to cut his paws. At first, the booties were awkward, so he walked funny, but after a few minutes he was fine with them. He is a big dog at ninety-two pounds and not agile. I knew his limitations. We worked what we could. At times, I would know he was too big for a certain search.

We worked with a group of firefighters and heavy machines that would scrape off a layer on the pile. Then Gondo would search. If he alerted, we would mark it, and the firefighters would come in to bag the remains. We would work for about thirty minutes, then the machines would scrape off another layer.

We worked twelve-hour days, but not constantly. There were laser sights on the building. If it seemed to be shifting, everyone would stop working until it was safe to do so. I have never associated with the families of victims, but there I could not avoid it. I was working with firefighters and it was their brother, or sister, or father, or uncle all buried in that pile. One of the firefighters told me his brother was inside the pile. That made it so much harder. Before going into the pile, I told them that Gondo gets a reward for his finds. We will look like a couple of idiots, but I will be screaming GOOD BOY and telling him what a great dog he is and also we would play with his toy. That is how he was trained, so that is how we work and how I keep him motivated so he will keep working. They told me to do whatever it took to keep him motivated and working. That was nice. We worked the pile, and when he alerted, I would be playing tug-of-war with him as the firefighters were uncovering the remains. The firefighters would begin to come up and play with him, too. It seemed he was almost doubling as a therapy dog during the down times. They would be hugging him and kissing him. That was very cool. Everyone wanted to pet him. He would sit there and give them kisses. Gondo found thirty-five little pieces of human remains. Nothing was recognizable, but with DNA work later, closure was given to some families.

At night, we would go back to the Helmsley Hotel that was housing workers for free. I would give him a bath and try to get down all that we had done that day. My truck would not fit in the parking garage, but the bellman told me to park on the road, and he would keep an eye on it. Gondo was popular in the hotel.

Dogs do not know they are finding dead people. They are trained to find a scent. They do not know it is a decomposing human. When I came home, people would often ask if Gondo was OK. Was he depressed? No, actually he was happy. He is a dog. In New York City, he did just what he is trained to do. Body parts do not depress him. No, he gave an alert and got his toy with each find, so he was a happy dog. Some may argue that dogs can smell death and be depressed. But I believe it is the handler who may get depressed, and that goes down the leash from the handler to the dog. The dog may then shut down.

I started working with the Cleveland FBI office right after 9/11. It was a sunny day; I was running with Gondo. We were in the local park in Willoughby Hills when my cell phone rang. It was the FBI. I was told the Wayne County sheriff had called to say they had an abduction of a fourteen-year-old girl. She had been walking home alone from the Wayne County Fair. They could not find her. Could I come with Gondo?

I ran home to change and took Gondo to the sheriff's office. They had a Jeep Cherokee for him to search. The owner had cleaned out the vehicle completely. It appeared as though he had taken a power wash from a drive-through car wash and sprayed the inside completely. The Jeep was in an enclosed place, so I could do a systematic search. The search is the same for police drug dogs as it is for a cadaver dog. The scent is the difference. The drug dogs alert on narcotics while cadaver dogs alert on human decomposition, but the training for searching is the same. I gave the command to Gondo, FIND THE DEAD.

I first worked on the outside of a car. All the doors were closed. My dog will sniff up and down the seams to see if they can alert to anything on the outside. Did not find anything on the outside. I opened all the car doors and the hatchback. Gondo went inside the Jeep to search. On the driver's side, nothing. Passenger side, nothing. Backseat, nothing. He went into the tailgate area sniffing along the plastic piece where the tailgate comes down and joins the D-post. His alert is to paw the area. He does not dig. If he cannot get to the place, he will bark. He began pawing and looking at me because he had found something and now wanted his reward of a jute rope. I looked, but I didn't see anything. The agents also looked without seeing anything. I know that sometimes all dogs will give a false alert because they are eager for their toy. But this time, Gondo was really pawing the post. The FBI began to search and found a tiny bit of flesh on the D-post. Later the lab test proved it to be from the missing fourteen-year-old girl. That linked the suspect with the victim. Three or four months later, the guy told authorities where her body was. This was a successful case. He confessed, but we already had the hard evidence that the girl had been in his Jeep. There was also a little bit of blood evidence in the Jeep. He had tried to wash it all away with the power wash, but he could not fool a dog! This case was so very sad and horrible, but finally the family did have closure.

People often do not seem to understand what we do with cadaver dogs. It is not only finding a whole body or evidence of that body; it is also finding blood splatter or bone fragments. My dogs alert on any human remains that have the scent of decomposing bodies. That is what they are trained for. K-9 Eliot can find a single tooth. Gondo has located a drop of blood on a stone in a gravel driveway. That is how sensitive their noses are. The big job is obviously to locate the body, so a family can have closure, but it is also to link the suspect to the victim to bring the criminal to justice. I have the only police cadaver dog in the whole northeastern Ohio area. There are cadaver dogs attached to volunteer search-and-rescue teams, but many police agencies do not know about them.

When I do drowning searches, my dog will alert to decomposition gases that rise to the surface. The dog never really sees the whole body. He will give an alert, then the divers come to recover the body. Some people think that maybe the dog dives into the water to bring the body to the surface. It doesn't work like that. When I work a case, I am able to disassociate myself. I do not deal with families. I do not inform the families. I am there to help by bringing closure and helping solve the crime. It must be so very difficult not to know what has happened to your loved one.

There was a drowning at a state park. A boat had run ashore without an operator. The port side rod and reel were missing. We did not know if the person was in the water or on land. We got into a search boat. Gondo was leaning over the edge of the boat sniffing, and alerted in one area. That area was then marked with small buoys. An underwater camera was used. The dive team found the rod and reel. Gondo had been a tracking dog first. He was a scent specific tracking dog. He knew live scent. I am not sure if Eliot could do that, he was never trained for live scent. The park rangers did not know if there was a body or not. When a dog comes out, he can save hours of time by letting authorities know yes, there is a drowning victim or no, there isn't. Then the dog's alert will give divers a general area in which to search, so they do not have to search expanses of water. Gondo was very good at finding drowning victims. I worked with him for eight-and-a-half years.

I have searched many huge Dumpsters with him. A Cleveland police officer called me. A lady had given birth in a hotel; her boyfriend disposed of the baby. Police thought the baby was in a Dumpster behind the hotel. The Dumpster had been searched, and nothing was found. I could climb into the Dumpster myself. Often the officers will help by taking the garbage out and spreading it on the ground for the dog to search. I was told to move on to other Dumpsters. I still felt we should search the first one again. Later they did re-search that same Dumpster and found the baby. The detective called to let me know that the baby was just where I had wanted to search! This has happened to me a couple of times; my instincts have told me that I should search something a second time, but officers will move me along.

One time, we followed a dump truck to the Harvard Transfer Station. They dump garbage into a pit and spread it around with a backhoe and then put into a bigger truck for a landfill. We did quite a bit of searching at the transfer station and went to the landfill. They knew which truck was the one we wanted to search, so we followed it. We were going through garbage and papers, and my dog got sick. I knew this was not good. I saw him chew a couple of things that I tried to grab out of his mouth. He later developed inflammatory bowel disease, and I always wondered if that had something to do with the landfill. I will no longer do landfills unless there is an exact location.

Ninety-five percent of my job is to clear areas. Then investigators can begin their work. They may have a tip: "There is a body there." So we go to clear the area. Yes, Gondo did alert, or no, he did not. I search in God knows what! I am working criminal cases and even here in the city, I just do not know what I may come across.

A call from a nearby city told me to go to a certain house to search. I needed to be added to the warrant to be able to search. I was told a female was missing. She lived there with her boyfriend. Her car was found down on the East 9th Street pier. Detectives thought something had happened in the house. It was very cluttered. Gondo did not show any interest on the second floor or downstairs. In the basement, there was a bedroom. A dog had been living there, and dog hair covered the floor, and clothes were scattered around. There was a bed and a dresser by the wall. It was not an easy search as the basement was so cluttered and full of dog smells. There were a couple of spots on the wall by the dresser. Gondo began barking at the wall. I took him around the room again, but when he got back to that wall, he began pawing at the corner of the dresser. It was an alert. Cuyahoga County Forensics Office took Luminal (a chemical that reacts with blood, making it glow) and put it on the wall and the dresser. Suddenly, glowing spots. A couple days later, she washed up onshore by the pier. Blood will soak into the walls. Even if someone would paint over blood spots, the dog can still sniff it out.

As one of the captains with Willoughby Hills Fire Department, I head one of the shifts. We do not do much with the dead from accidents. That is the job of the county coroner. I do observe and let him know what I have observed. After working with him for years, he trusts my opinion. After I retire as a firefighter, I should have learned enough to be a coroner's investigator and do something full-time with cadaver dogs. Yes, I do love my job.

Day-to-Day Patrolling

Trooper Drew Griffith

(September 22, 1961–April 15, 1996)
Maine State Police, Thomaston, Maine
K-9 ROCK

Trooper Griffith formerly worked for the U.S. Capitol Police in Washington, D.C. He moved to Maine to work as an undercover narcotics officer for the Maine Drug Enforcement Agency. He later joined Troop D and began training as a K-9 handler with four-year-old shepherd Rock. Drew had young children of his own and enjoyed giving many presentations to the schoolchildren in Knox County.

My daughter Beth used to babysit for Drew's four children. She often told me how she enjoyed being with the whole family. She knew of my deep interest in police work dogs. One day, she called in tears. Drew had just been killed on patrol. While in pursuit of a speeder, he made a U-turn and was hit broadside by a truck. K-9 Rock was not seriously injured. Several years later, I met Kate to find out how she was coping without her beloved Drew. Drew's wife, now his widow, told me the following gentle and very loving story.

Drew's close friend Trooper Billy Smith always had a deal going. If anything would ever happen to Drew, Billy would try to get K-9 Rock out of the car. The second solution was to call me. If anyone would ever get near the police car, Rock would go bananas. So this was always a real issue. That day, Billy was actually on his way home to Thomaston from Portland. He was listening to the scanner in his car. He heard Drew sign on. He tried to contact him to arrange a meeting but could not make contact. Then he heard the scanner traffic about the accident. He kept waiting for Drew to come back on. Instead, he heard, "The dog is still in the car and very agitated." He heard the dispatcher say to do whatever was needed to get the dog out of the car, so paramedics could get to the officer. Billy's first thought was that they might shoot Rock. He began racing toward the accident.

When he arrived, he found that Rock was in the rear seat cage, but could get his head through. Rock seemed to be thinking he should bite the paramedic who was trying to find Drew's vital signs. He did know his partner was in trouble, but he did not know what to do. He seemed to know he should not attack the paramedic. Fire Chief Tyler came up to the cruiser and opened the door. Rock stopped barking. He was put into the chief's car. Rock was only slightly injured; he was taken to Lakeview Veterinary Hospital to be treated for a bruised hip. He stayed there for the week of the funeral.

Drew had said, "Rock is not afraid of anything. He will never stop in the middle of crises to ask if he had made the right career choice. He simply reacts instinctively and unhesitatingly. He provides unquestioning and loving companionship for me." Drew was often training Rock, as good enough was not good enough. He kept working for higher standards. He worked with the other handlers and assisted in rewriting the training manual. Drew died doing the work he loved as a Maine state trooper and K-9 handler.

I had always imagined that my life would stop upon hearing the words *your husband is dead*. What could possibly follow? What followed was life.

A few months after Drew died, I wanted to drive to Washington, D.C., to visit my mother. At first, I hesitated, as two of the children had fevers and were vomiting. The other two did not get sick, so with a lot of ginger ale we decided to go. When we got to Newburyport, we saw the Massachusetts State Police Barracks. The kids begged me to stop. I thought that would be a good idea, and we could use the bathrooms. The kids wanted to talk to the troopers. After we introduced ourselves, they gave us a tour of the whole facility. They gave the kids stuffed animals and said we must have a sleeve patch. The trooper ripped one right off of his uniform. We really understood that we would be a part of the police family forever.

While I was visiting my mother on her horse farm, I stepped on a dung fork that went right through my foot. I wound up six days in the hospital with an IV drip of antibiotics. I was not sure I could drive myself and four children back to Maine. Luckily, Drew's close friend Billy Smith offered to fly down and drive us home.

In Brunswick, Maine, we stopped for gas. Bill asked if I saw the truck over there. It was the one with the gold-colored cab. It belonged to the same company as the truck that hit Drew. I had not seen a picture of the ice truck. It looked bigger than I would have imagined, and the cab was an odd color of gold. Whoever heard of a gold ice truck? While I paid for the gas, Bill found the driver and asked about the other guy, the one who crashed into the trooper. The driver said, "That was me. I was the one." Bill told him that the trooper's wife and children were here, and it would probably be all right to speak to me if he wanted to. The next thing I knew, the driver approached me. His face was sorrowful and decent. He was evidently a good young man. I hugged him briefly and told him I was glad to meet him. Conversation was awkward but not painful. He went back to his truck. I began to cry. Bill also started to cry, and I looked back at the truck. The driver was crying, too.

How could this be? I came to Maine on a beautiful day, and the first person I speak with is the driver of the truck that killed my Drew. And that driver was a decent soul, sweet-faced and sad. I cannot answer my own questions. I couldn't make sense of it rationally or explain why, despite my tears, the meeting had been comforting. I had the feeling it had been a sign or gift from Drew tying up one more sad little loose end, so I could keep on living in this life that won't let me do otherwise. And this was comforting, too. To think that if Drew did turn his head at that last final moment he would have seen in the pure dazzling morning light a guy with the face of an angel at the wheel of a bright gold truck.

This is the letter I wrote:

Dear all of you Maine state troopers in your handsome blue uniforms with all your shiny leather gear and your good, brave hearts, I am sorry that the thanks given here cannot be more complete. I could fill pages with my gratitude and might well name you all. Maine is so fortunate to have all of you in her service. I was the very fortunate wife of a Maine state trooper. I am now the honored widow. Our four children are Zach, Peter, Ellie, and Woolie.
Yours, Kate Braestrop Griffith

Two short stories about my Drew. One time he had to go after a drunk. They knew the guy would probably bail out and run into the woods. It was dark and raining. He did run into a cow field, and they followed with Rock. They began to track the suspect when they heard a thumping noise behind them. They turned around and saw a gigantic bull pawing the ground and looking right at them. Immediately, the deputy and Rock ran behind Drew. Rock seemed to be saying, "I am not going to deal with this." Drew thought that it would be stupid to die being gored by a bull who was clearly about to act. He had no idea if a bullet would even slow down a huge bull. So they all ran and were able to get through the barbed-wire fence. The bad guy probably got home safely that night. Drew decided to pretend the whole incident had not happened.

Another night, Drew stopped for a bottle of milk on his way home. In the parking lot, he recognized a man wanted for gross sexual misconduct. Drew arrested him, handcuffed him, and put him in the front seat of the police car. Rock was in the back growling and shaking his head, so slobber was going all over the prisoner. The prisoner asked if the dog would bite him. Drew said, "The dog will bite if I tell him to." Rock turned around and around in the backseat of the car and finally plopped down. He let go with a terrible smell that filled the car. The prisoner asked if this was a violation of his constitutional rights. Drew would not open the windows, but pretended he did not notice anything. The prisoner arrived at the jail covered in slime and smelling like dog poop.

K-9 Rock wanted to work. He was not happy as a home dog. K-9 Rock eventually served at the Maine Correctional Center in South Windham.

Deputy Bob Tucker

Manatee County Sheriff's Office, Manatee County, Florida

K-9 TESSA

At the beginning of a two-week training session, I had been intro-
duced to the handlers as a writer interested in taping their stories
for a book. We were all staying at the same motel. Each morning,
the parking lot would be filled with men walking their dogs. Bob
stopped briefly to say he had a story I must hear. When there was
a lull in training, Bob asked me to sit on the grass beside Tessa.
He told me about the night he and Tessa were crushed between
two patrol cars. I almost felt as though my tape recorder was an
invasion of privacy. I heard the story of a dog's total devotion to
her handler.

It was July; I was answering a burglary call with my dog, Tessa. I had
turned off the lights and parked my car on a dirt road about a thousand
feet from the house. I was waiting for the perimeter to be set when I called
her to me. I had opened the back of the truck to get her tracking lead. One
of the backup officers was coming down the street approximately 15 to
17 mph with his lights off. He did not see me. Tessa and I were crushed
between the two cars.

I had just finished obedience training with her, so she still had her
hard metal pinch collar with prongs on it. When the call came for the
burglary, I went hot to the call and had not bothered to take that collar off.
The collar was crushed flat! She had a chipped tooth, broken left shoulder,
lacerations on the other shoulder, and a rib had punctured a lung. Tessa's
forehead was sliced, and her tongue was split. I have no idea and neither
does the vet or anyone else who saw the wreckage know how she could
still be alive. I had put her in a SIT/STAY, so she was completely at knee
level when we got nailed. The only thing that saved her life was my left
leg between her and the bumper of the car. Her head was in that gap.

This was supposed to be a burglary in progress, and we had parked away from the house, so we could walk up on them. Just to be tactical, we would not pull up to the front door only to have him run out the back. We wanted to catch him in the house.

I had compound tibia and fibula fractures in both legs. One leg was almost severed below my knee; the only thing that was hanging on was probably about two fingers wide part of my calf.

The officer who had hit us freaked out when he saw us. Tessa was spinning around on the ground trying to get up, but her shoulder was dislocated, so she couldn't. When it did finally pop back into place, she came and lay on my chest and began guarding me. Her split tongue was heavily bleeding all over me. I finally calmed her down and put her off to the side. I thought she was going to die. My legs were lying all over the place around me. My radio had been crushed, and we were in a dead area, so we did not have communications. One of my legs looked like roadkill, just pieces with the bones sticking out. I thought it was gone.

I had to lie in the rain for an hour waiting for a flight to the hospital. I do not remember the first three days in the hospital, but the first thing I said when I woke up was, "Where is my dog?" I did not remember all of what had happened. Tessa was being cared for at the veterinarian hospital.

The surgeons did a wonderful job putting me back together. When they said I would lose my leg, I said, "B.S. There is no way!" My leg got infected. They wanted to amputate it. I told the doctor he should have amputated my leg when he had a chance, because he wasn't going to do it now! I told him there were not enough hospital employees to hold me down. So they pumped me full of antibiotics and gave me a week. I was even told if I kept the leg I could probably not use it. The doctors said if I kept my leg I might walk but never run and would have to use a cane the rest of my life. I had five or six surgeries and ended up with titanium rods in both legs.

I was in the hospital for thirty days. One day, the major and other officers brought Tessa to the hospital, sneaking her onto the elevator. She began air-scenting while on the elevator. She broke loose from them and ran to my room. She had scented me and ran right to me and jumped up onto the orthopedic chair. She lay right on my chest! She began licking me as though she would never leave. She would go into a defensive mode if they tried to take her off me. This dog had been crushed between two cars, but her only concern was "Where is my daddy?" She had never been in a hospital before, but she was amazing. She showed such a display of partnership. She seemed to know that something was going on with my legs, so she stayed on my chest. When it was time for her to leave, she growled as though to say, "I Am Not Going." I told her it was OK. But still they had to drag her down the hallway while I cried.

Twenty days later, I was home. My dad would wheel me outside with Tessa. I would throw the Kong for her to chase. She would bring it back to me. She knew I could not chase her. Her best obedience was during the time I was in the wheelchair. She would heel as it went down the ramp, just like a guide dog.

I went to see Sheriff Charlie Wells and said, "Tessa is too young to just sit around with me. I don't want her to go to waste; you might think of giving her to another handler." I knew she belonged to the sheriff's office; she wasn't my dog.

The sheriff said she was my dog. "And when you choose to come back to work, you will work with your dog."

I wore a brace and worked at a desk for a while. Tessa came to work with me each day, and I trained her in narcotics since we could not patrol. Limited duty, it was called. I did that for two years.

They put me back together pretty well. The pain is always terrible, but I made it back to the SWAT team. I run funny, I look funny, but I can run and keep up with everyone. Everyone in the department knows how much I love dogs and always have. We are back on the road now. We both have limps and scars. My unit is Manatee County in South Florida. Tessa has found hundreds of pounds of dope. We have limited apprehensions because we have been off the road so long, but the number is still more than forty. I am a trainer now. Tessa will lay on your lap, lick your face, or rip your arm off—whatever I ask her to do.

At the accident, I was lying on the ground with my leg here and there, and I did not know what was going to happen to me. My major responded. I have a good rapport with him as we were together on the SWAT team for eight years. I looked up at him and asked, "Why?" I was a SWAT team sniper, K-9 team, and dive team member. I was probably one of the most active handlers they ever had. I was physically fit—now what was going to happen? My sheriff was so very supportive. Through the whole healing process, Tessa was with me. I went to the pharmacy for pain medication. The pharmacist helped me with workers' compensation paperwork and my insurance.

Then the sheriff's office assigned me to pharmacy fraud. I would find a bad script and go to the pharmacy to track it down. There she was again, the pharmacist. I fell in love! So my question to the major the day of the accident was "Why?" And the answer was, to meet my future wife! If I had not had the accident, I might still be on the road running around like a banshee chasing the bad guys. I turned my wife into a dog person. God had to slow me down long enough to find a wife.

I am thirty-eight years old, and there are no part-time dog handlers. You either love the job, or you are not a handler. If I were a millionaire, I would still love this job. If I were told I was no longer needed, and Tessa could no longer be my partner, she would suddenly disappear. I would paint her black and hide her in the attic.

Postscript: This is my story of K-9 Tessa. She was my partner for two-and-a-half years. She was one-and-a-half years old at the time of the accident. She has earned her retirement. She is nine years old now and is enjoying it at home with my wife and me. Yes, she is retired and MINE! When my wife and I are lounging around watching TV, the other dogs in the family are also lounging with us, but Tessa will stand in the middle of the room like a bold statue staring at me sometimes for as long as ten minutes as if to say, "Are you really safe? May I lay down, too?"

Officer Dave Crespin

Torrance Police Department, Torrance, California
K-9 CONDOR

Dave was no longer a K-9 handler when I met him, but very active with Community Affairs and an instructor for the Torrance Citizens Police Academy. As a graduate of Shaker Heights Citizens Police Academy, I am always interested to attend a class in another town when I know the instructor. Dave proudly took me to meet the new Torrance K-9s.

One evening at the end of my shift, I stopped to buy a take-out dinner at a Chinese restaurant. On my way home, I got out of the car to issue a traffic ticket. When I came back to my car, K-9 Condor was looking very guilty. The Styrofoam take-out box was in shreds all over the seats. Condor had Chinese noodles hanging from his mouth.

There was a break-in at a department store after hours. The alarm had sounded. I was sent to check it out. The store owner also arrived at the scene. I did not know if the burglar was still inside. I gave Condor the command FIND HIM! I could hear the sound of his collar and his claws on the polished floor. Then there was silence. Condor, in his excitement, had pooped right in the middle of a priceless Oriental rug. I was never so embarrassed. It was all my fault as I had forgotten to give him a break before I sent him into the store. The owner was most gracious in forgiving us.

There was another break-in. Condor was given the command FIND HIM! He ran around the store without giving an alert. He could not find anyone inside. He must have been mystified by a mannequin who looked real but wasn't. Condor returned to me with the dummy's wig in his mouth. He had done the best he could.

I was outside of the police car during a traffic stop. The driver of the car I had stopped began to get rough. Condor could not exit the car, but he kept trying to get out to help me. He leaped from the backseat to the front seat, hitting the windshield with his nose. When I got back into the car, there was a streak of blood down the windshield where he had hit with great force. He really wanted to protect me.

Corporal Tim Keck

Shaker Heights Police Department, Shaker Heights, Ohio
K-9s BLITZ AND ARGUS

Many of the handlers from nearby towns take turns as host to plan the twice-a-month training days. The sites differ to give the dogs varied training. Sometimes the site might begin in a metro park and then move to an abandoned Howard Johnson's motel to find hidden drugs. I was invited to many of those days. One day, the training site was by the narrow part of the Chagrin River. One by one, the dogs were commanded to TRACK AND FIND a "suspect" hidden in a tree across the river. The dogs really seemed to enjoy the swim. They ran to the tree and began barking, signaling their handler that they had found the suspect.

Chief Peter Gray wanted to start a K-9 program. They got approval for one dog, and I ended up with it. I was one of six candidates. I thought it would be exciting to work with a dog, though I had never worked a dog in my life. I did have one as a pet. I did a lot of research for the K-9 unit. I went to different towns to talk with handlers and watch them work. Another officer and I went to get my dog. He was so scraggly looking. I hoped he was not the one chosen for me. The trainer handed me the leash, and that dog almost pulled me out the door. He was full of piss and vinegar, and we took him home. The first thing he did was to walk up to my wife's laundry basket of clean clothes and pee all over it. I tried to discipline him, and he bit me! That would be the last time. I grabbed his neck and disciplined him for many minutes and threw him outside to do his business. Never again did he even raise his lip at me or growl again. If I looked at him when he was wrong, he just put his head down.

Blitz was a purebred German shepherd and a very green dog. He rode with me for a week before we went to school together. He became acclimated with the department. I kept him on a leash as I did not know the Czech commands, and I didn't want to screw him up. Blitz was trained with voice commands in Czech, but I soon taught him commands in English.

There was a raid on Sutton Road about 3 a.m. The suspect jumped through a third-floor window, hit a tree, did a somersault, and took off running. The cops lost him, so they called me to bring Blitz. I told them I don't know what in hell I am doing. I do not know what this dog can do! They said just bring him out of the freaking car. I did. It was springtime, so no footprints in snow. We went to the front of the house where we lost the guy. My dog was on a long lead. He stopped and sniffed some bushes, raised his leg, and we hear "Cut it out!" My dog was peeing all over the suspect hidden in the flowerbed under some evergreens. We got the suspect, and my dog was not even working yet. That was hilarious. The guy smelled pretty bad.

We began school together in September and graduated in December. It was freezing cold when we practiced tracking in the snow. We practiced at least eight hours a day, sometimes until 10 p.m., and we still had more then an hour drive home. Since I was the first, the department did not own a K-9 equipped car. I built a platform for the back and had a screen welded. As we drove, Blitz would put his head through the mesh wire. When we graduated, there was a big ceremony with the mayor and a lot of hoopla. Then we went on the road.

There was a burglar working the Scottsdale Road area. He would kick in a door to steal a purse. If he encountered anyone, he would assault the person by pushing him or her in the face. We knew who he was. There was a warrant for his arrest. He had just committed another burglary in another town; there was a big vehicle pursuit. The guy bailed out, shot at an officer, and took off down a hill. We lost sight of him. I was called out with Blitz. I took him to the suspect's car to begin a track. Blitz tracked right down the hillside to the third house on the street. He pulled me right up to the back door. I took him to the backyard, but he went right back to the door. I told the officers that the suspect was in this house. I said I hated to tell them, but the suspect isn't going anywhere. He is in this house. They swore up and down. I said I would stand right there while they looked around. Blitz was right beside me; the house next door hid us. The window on the second floor opened and this *schlemiel* comes crawling out onto the roof. He saw me and went back into the house.

I called the officers and told them, but they still did not believe me. It turned out to be a seven-hour stand off with the SWAT team there with *Mother* (the name for their armored car), but still the guy would not give up. Finally, they gassed the house. He was found in the rafters in the attic. He had been so badly gassed that they had to strip him naked and wrap him in blanket because he smelled so much of gas. That was my first good apprehension. Blitz did not get a bite, but he took me right to the guy. Later the officers told me I had done a good job. I thought to myself, *Then why didn't you believe me the first time?*

One night, I was working in an unmarked car on midnight shift. Blitz and I used to work 7 p.m. to 3 a.m. and I really liked that shift. I was on patrol while roll call was still going on at the station about 11 p.m. I tried to make a traffic stop on a New York car, but it would not stop. We were in pursuit until we got to a shopping center at Harvard and Lee Roads. I did not have a backup as they were still in roll call being assigned duties for their shifts. I knew the car was stolen. The guy got out of the car. I tried to get him to get back in the car or get down on the ground. He would not do either. He kept trying to get a key into the lock to open the car door. I kept telling him to lie down on the ground. Blitz jumped out of my unmarked car barking and growling. The guy saw my dog. He yelled, "Whoow!" and lay flat down on the ground. My backup was arriving. I looked inside the stolen car; there on the front seat was a six-inch Magnum fully loaded. I took the guy back to the station. He told me if he could have unlocked his car I would be dead. He said he had every intention of killing me. I asked him why he didn't. "The dog! That is what saved you. I did not know you had a dog until he jumped out of the car; otherwise, I was going to shoot you."

Back in the 1980s, I used Blitz for crowd control. There used to be a problem with kids having large parties. There were two hundred or more kids at a time causing havoc. As the parties would break up, the fights would begin. Five guys cannot handle that many kids. I would bring my dog out, and the street would clear much quicker and without pepper gas. Blitz would be on a fifteen-foot lead, barking and growling, and immediately the area would be cleared. We had ten or eleven of those incidents.

One night, there was a burglar working on the west side of our town. We knew he would strike again, so all the detective bureau and

SWAT were out. A detective saw two schmucks crawl into a window. We could not unlock a door, so I lifted Blitz through a window. He ran right upstairs. The guys heard him coming and were in a panic mode trying to figure out a way to either get out or away from my dog. They crawled out onto a ledge. Blitz stayed barking at the window. We got one off the ledge and put him on the ground. I told him. "Spread your legs. Do not move!" I brought Blitz down and put him between the suspect's spread legs. The other guy had climbed onto the roof; a detective grabbed for him, but he pulled away and fell three floors. He lived! During the commotion, Blitz got excited and the suspect flinched. He had moved, so Blitz bit him in a very tender spot.

Yes, this life is hard on families of an officer. There are always things I do not tell my wife about my career. She pretty much lets me do my job as far as being a police officer. She was an investigator with RTA (the local transit company), and that is how I met her. She raises the kids, and I bring home the bacon. She does not worry (she says), but accepts my job as an officer. I am getting a bit old to ride the streets, but I still do it. I just love my job. I have been in law enforcement for twenty-eight years and still want to stay another five or six. The benefits outweigh the bad times.

Officer Kenneth Greenleaf

Redondo Beach Police Department, Redondo Beach, California
K-9s BORIS, ASKO, BASKO, AND VALOR

This was how I learned never to take a cup of steaming hot coffee into a cruiser. Ken had invited me to ride on patrol one evening. We stopped at coffee shop. Suddenly, he received a radio call to domestic disturbance. We grabbed the coffee and sprinted to his cruiser. He went to the disturbance. I stayed in the car with Asko. Somehow my thumb poked a hole in the Styrofoam cup. Coffee began to pour into my lap. I tried to drink it quickly, but it was too hot. I tried to open the cruiser window, but they were lock-controlled. When Ken came back, I had locked him out of the cruiser and did not know how to get the door open. There was a big puddle of coffee on the floor. In spite of the mess, Ken continued to invite me to ride on patrol with him, and together with Basko, we gave a demo at El Retiro Library.

My first dog, Boris, was the youngest K-9 the RBPD (Redondo Beach Police Department) had ever hired. One night, Boris caught his first burglary suspect. The guy was climbing over a fence. Boris grabbed his leg. I was yelling *PLACKEN! PLACKEN!* which means "take hold of." But the suspect thought I was telling Boris to let go! The burglar started yelling *PLACKEN! PLACKEN!* He thought he was telling Boris to let go. I still laugh at that.

When Boris would bark, there was a reason for it. He would bark for a second and stop. One time, he kept barking while I was patting down a guy. I said to myself, *Something is wrong here—Boris never keeps barking.* The guy seemed very nice, but I found a long knife stuck down his pants. How did my dog know? The guy was nervous; he sensed I would find the knife; his scent blew into Boris's face. When a person is nervous, he gives off a different smell.

It is said a K-9 can learn 150 commands. I have heard an officer say that when he talks to his dog the dog only hears *blah, blah, blah.* That cannot be true. When I say SIT, he sits. If I say *PLOTZ*, he lays down, so he does hear and does understand. My dogs have worked a lot by the tone of my voice. There was an incident where a guy was hiding under a car. The dog found him and was just going to sit there and bark. Someone said something in English like GET HIM, and the dog seemed to know what was meant. He dove under the car and dragged the guy out.

Some ask why we give certain commands in German. We do it because people think it is cool. K-9 cops think it is cool, too.

We do helicopter training to prepare a K-9 in case we must use a helicopter. What I am trying to do in training—and a dog is never fully trained—is to be prepared if a child gets lost and the only way to find the child is in a helicopter. Some dogs might freak out. What would happen in the air if the dog freaks out and hits the controls? My dog loves to ride; some dogs don't but will get used to it. I also teach him to go up and down children's slides and places where the footing is bad, like gratings. I also take him on rocks in the ocean. I do constant training, so my dogs can work in different situations.

I train our dogs to scent four narcotics. Asko can smell five: marijuana, tar heroin, cocaine, opium, and methamphetamine. Dogs do not sniff and smell something as humans do. We see people and things, but a dog uses his nose. He can smell four or five odors of drugs and remember them. When a person goes into the kitchen, he can smell beef stew as one odor. The dogs smell the meat, the onions, the carrots, the peas, the garlic, and whatever is in the stew; they smell separately. The dogs never get used to an odor as we do. When our dogs search, they are looking for their toy. They think their toy is hidden.

Dogs don't find narcotics; they find the odor of narcotics. If marijuana is removed from a bag and the bag resealed, there will still be the odor inside, so my dog with still alert on it.

I love working with dogs. It keeps me active. Some handlers think they are very good, but they know absolutely nothing. I am the opposite. I think I know hardly anything. One key is watching other people work and train, so you can pick and choose what you will use. Handlers have one thing in common: We all love our dogs. There is a saying that sounds a little awkward, but it is true. "You can make fun of my wife or girlfriend—but don't ever make fun of my dog."

All dogs should always be under control. It is for the safety of the dog, which comes first. If he is chasing someone and is about to run across a busy street, you need to be able to call him off. He should immediately stop. Perhaps you might have sent your dog after the wrong person. Will he stop when you command him? Dogs are trained to apprehend suspects, but you need to be able to control the dog and also be aware of his safety. Dogs are trained to apprehend suspects, but the handler does not always think about the safety of the dog. Now and then we have had a burglary suspect play with the dog after they have been arrested.

Dogs very rarely hold a grudge. Rarely, but it does happen. During a K-9 trial, a handler accidentally stepped on his dog's paw. The shepherd let out loud, heartbreaking yelps, fell on his side, and held his temporarily injured paw curled in the air. The dog actually recovered quickly and got back at his handler by defecating on the course. That disqualified him. The trials are not to see which dog is the best, but so law enforcement can demonstrate their K-9 programs to one another and to the public.

When I had reports to write, I would go to the park and let Boris out to play. I always knew he was still out there because the back car door was open. One day, the door was shut and I went on a call and then back to the station. I called to him COME ON, but no dog. I had been to the park and several other places, so now I had to remember where I left him. I went to the park and yelled. . . . Nothing! I began to panic. I went around the full block of the park, but no dog. I decided to try one more time before I would call anyone to help. And there he was in the middle of the park, sitting there. I called him and wanted to give him a hug, but he ran right past me and jumped into the car.

Redondo Beach has 104 officers on its force; we cover eight square miles with about sixty-five thousand residents. On a summer day, we have over two hundred thousand a day. I do not write many traffic tickets, maybe one a month if someone isn't lucky. They have to be very bad for me to write a ticket. It is funny that most people who are wanted by the police have something stupid wrong with their car—a taillight out or an expired license. When I stop them, I listen to what the driver is saying; sometimes it sounds weird. Then I check and find the driver has outstanding warrants.

The purpose of the RBPD K-9 Program is to deter the crime element within the city. When criminals see our dogs, they know there is no escape. As the saying goes, "You can run, but you cannot hide." We do sell T-shirts, but none of ours features a dog being aggressive. Some have the logo "Put Teeth into the Law," but the photo shows happy dogs. We do not show the teeth; we want to be more positive.

Most dogs work about six years from age two to eight. Boris lasted eight full years.

These dogs retire when they cannot work anymore. If I am running after a suspect in an alley and I get there first, it is time to retire them. They usually die within a year of retiring, so that is why we let them work as long as they can. Bred to work, love to work, so we let them. When they retire, we can buy them from the city for a dollar, and they become ours to keep comfortable at home.

When I had to retire my second dog, it was not as hard as it could have been. I knew he was getting too old to work, and I also knew I would be getting Basko. It was easier then when I retired Boris. Then I did not know I was going to have another dog. All of my dogs have loved staying in the car. I do not think it is just that they want to work, but it is security for them and that way they know you cannot leave without them.

When the dog trusts his handler, he has confidence that whatever he is told will be OK. If I tell him to HUP, which means to jump, he knows "My dad told me to jump and I won't get hurt." Obstacle courses teach this.

I like to photograph my dogs. Each year, there is a competition; I try to get new photos. One year, I had Boris standing by an SPCA truck with the guy in an SPCA uniform with his hands up as though being arrested—with Boris barking at him.

My dogs are dogs, and I treat them like dogs. I give them plenty of loving. Each of my dogs has had a different personality. Boris and Asko are probably two of the best-known dogs in the South Bay area. In my car, I have a padded part between the two front seats, so Basko can come up and put his head in my lap, and I can pet him often. Many handlers keep their dog in the back of the cruiser and keep the screen shut. I let mine come up and put his head on my leg, and I pet him as we drive along.

I have searched a car when my dog has alerted, but cannot find any drugs. I tell the driver, "My dog has alerted, but I do not see anything,

I am not going to arrest you." He will reply, "Oh yeah, I did have drugs there last week."

Dogs can get so tired and bored that they might false alert. A handler can tell his dog to alert. Lay people do not realize an officer can make a dog bark at certain things, and the dog will, but has no clue why he is doing it.

If we are searching and my voice changes, that could key my dog into alerting: "Oh, my handler changed his tone of voice." You have to be careful that you let the dog search and you don't search for him in training. If he comes near the hidden evidence and you begin to say GOOD DOG, he learns to bark and give an alert when really you have told him where it is. That is a major problem with handlers.

When I train at night, I never use a flashlight. It bugs me when other officers use a flashlight. None of our RBPD handlers uses one. The reason is you are teaching the dog to go where the light is, while what you want is for the dog to search and sniff and use his nose. Obviously, on the street, you have to use a light, but if you have done training, the dog on the street will ignore the light. Those are little key things that make a well-trained dog a better dog. We have to be careful when packaging drugs for training that we package them differently. There is the chance you are teaching your dog to alert on your own scent. He needs not to search for human scent, but for narcotics. One training day, we had a big bank of lockers, and in each I put something different: coffee (dogs love the smell of coffee), dog biscuits, some personal items like a wallet—everything I could think of, but no drugs at all. Some were in plastic bags, some in foil. When the handlers came through the exercise with their dogs, if the dog found something, it was wrong. We have to train like that. We proof the dog, making sure he is only alerting to narcotics. Some people think all money is tainted with narcotics. That is not true.

My dog alerts by scratching, not barking. If I had it to do over, I would have him be passive, not scratch but simply sit down by the narcotic. He only barks when he finds a person. The barking can scare a suspect to give up, but there is no reason to bark on narcotics. It isn't going anywhere. Dogs should learn to be quiet when you want them to be quiet. When we first got our young dogs, they had no clue how to find narcotics or find a person. We would put out several large boxes with a person hiding in one of the boxes. The dog would scratch at that box as he had first learned to find narcotics and knew to scratch. I had to teach him to back off the box and just bark. Now he knows the difference. If I tell him FIND IT, that is the command for drug search. If I tell him SEARCH, he knows he is looking for a person.

While I cannot say my dog has saved my life, he has told me when other people are around that I did not know about.

I am a true believer that I must not expect my dog to find everything he looks for. In drug searches, the odor could be so faint or the air blowing one way while he is searching the other way. Or a dog can exhale when he should be inhaling; so many things can go wrong. We as officers have to search every day. We look for people and cannot find them. Why do we think a dog should find everything?

My K-9 Basko was conducting a training search for narcotics when he found cocaine under a refrigerator. As it sometimes happens, Basko was able to get to the narcotics and bit through a puncture-proof sack. We did not know at the time that Basko had ingested some of the cocaine, as he continued searching and found seven more training aids perfectly. Within twenty minutes of that first find, Basko went into cardiac arrest and died on the way to the vet clinic. As I was driving Basko to the emergency room, somehow he made his way between the seats and was able to put his full mouth around my right arm and hold on without biting down. He then went to sleep. He was a great dog and will always be remembered.

From the *Daily Breeze* newspaper:

Hundreds gather to honor fallen Redondo Beach canine. Dozens of dogs wailed mournfully as the sun started to set and a bagpipe began its melancholy tune. Dogs and their handlers came from police departments across Southern California to say good-bye to one of their own. "We did everything together," Greenleaf said. "He was always there." Basko was named after the two dogs Greenleaf previously worked with, Boris and Asko.

Narcotics

Detective Gene Cook

East Cleveland Police Department, East Cleveland, Ohio

K-9 GUNNER

Gunner is a narcotics-trained dog. On training days while other K-9 teams were practicing aggression or tracking, Gene had time to tell me about Gunner. He joked that his next pet would be a goldfish, but I did not believe him. Like many police K-9s, when Gunner is not working, he is a lovable dog who likes to have his ears softly petted or to lean against me as I talked with Gene. Gene has a great sense of both humor and compassion.

Sometimes I wonder if I train Gunner or if he trains me. When he finds narcotics, I give him a reward—a rolled-up terrycloth towel for a tug-of-war. Maybe Gunner thinks he is training me to give him the reward.

Gunner is not a patrol dog. He knows obedience or what is convenient for him. He knows his job and that is what he prefers to do. He does love other animals. We were doing a drug search. As we were going down a hallway, a mother cat jumped out and tried to get Gunner to chase her. She was trying to lead him away from her newborn kittens. We have a cat at home, so this was not a big deal for him. The kittens saw him and began crawling up his legs. They tried to grab his wagging tail to play with. Gunner was trying to do his job of sniffing for drugs, so he kicked the kittens off his legs. They kept running back as though he was the neatest play toy. The room was very clean, and it seemed obvious there weren't any drugs in there. Gunner was off leash. Each time he would finish searching a room, he would run back to check on the kittens. It was surprising to see the mothering instincts come out in this male dog. He was so very concerned for those tiny newborns. He did find the hidden dope and got his reward of the towel, which he then took back to the baby kittens, to be with them until the mother cat returned.

We do many school demos. I let the kids do a lot of hands-on. They hide the drugs for my dog to find and they play tug-of-war with him. He has not been taught aggression at all. He just loves little kids. I sometimes let the kids circle around my dog, but I make sure they do not yank on him. I pass out a pen-and-ink drawing of a paw print. It says: Just Say No to Drugs.

A couple weeks later, I was in the same city assisting with a search warrant. When the apartment was secure and safe for my dog to search, we went in. There in the living room were two kids, an older male, and a woman. One of the little kids jumped off the couch, ran to Gunner, and hugged him. He said to Gunner, "Where have you been? I have been asking for you to come here." Later I found my pen-and-ink drawing in the little boy's bedroom. We took his older brother to jail for possession. I felt so bad.

I was talking to third, fourth, and fifth graders. I held up a blunt. That is a hollowed-out cigar filled with marijuana. I asked them if they knew what it was. They all knew. So sad what so many kids have been exposed to.

Another time, we were doing a search warrant at a two-story house. It was a nice day, and the windows were open, so they saw us and the SWAT team coming. As fast as we were, they still had time to hide the dope. We secured the house and took the dog upstairs to search. No alerts. I went into the bathroom. My dog alerts to the toilet, right around the bowl area and the floor by the wax ring. I opened the lid of the toilet, and the dog was going nuts. This is when I get to utilize my seniority. I called one of the officers over saying, "My dog alerted on the toilet." The officer looked inside, "I don't see nothing." I told him I did not see anything, either, but my dog alerted here. He told me to put my hand down there. I told him, "My job is the dog; your job is to look where I tell you to look."

The officer went into the bedroom for a wire coat hanger. He poked it down the toilet and felt something. He pokes a bit harder. Oh! We see all this brown stuff come up, not feces but powder. He dives into the toilet; there is a little over a pound of heroin stuck in the neck of the toilet. The bad guy had the dope in his hand. When he shoved it into the neck of the toilet, he had his other hand on the bowl of the toilet. Gunner alerted to the scent on the toilet bowl. We were searching the house within seconds of arriving, so he had very little time to hide it. Did the dog alert to dope inside the water? He had alerted where the hand had been on the toilet.

The dog knows where the dope has been; it is almost like a dead scent.

We are finding a lot of the dope that is coming in now in seal-a-meal bags. This makes me understand that these products are not all that good. The bags shrink-wrap food. The dogs can smell drugs in those bags. It is very funny. I got a sealed meal bag with the dope inside with paper towels, liquid soap, and mustard, everything was sucked down inside. I opened it with my knife; it expanded with air. All the mustard and soap exploded out. The dogs alert to it. I tell everyone if they don't want the dog to alert to drugs to put the drugs in a white terry-cloth towel. My dog's reward is a white terry-cloth towel. I tell anyone who will listen, the best way to hide dope is in a white terry-cloth towel. Laughter.

Working with Gunner to find drugs is like hide-and-seek; it is so much fun. That is why I have been doing it for so long. That is why I still do it. I have a dog that is better than I am. We did a search warrant a couple of Fridays ago. There are not a lot of K-9s in this area that are certified in ecstasy, but Gunner is. I was called to do an ecstasy warrant. I told him to do his tricks, and he did. He came up with a bunch of money and a bunch of ecstasy.

We finished upstairs. I was standing at the top of the steps and sent him down. I thought he would wait for me. There were people downstairs that he knew and he must have thought, *The old man is still upstairs and it will take him forever, so I will go visiting.* The bad guys were in there, too, all handcuffed. Guess Gunner thought they couldn't be all that bad because they were with people I knew. He was being very friendly. All I heard was screaming! And howling! I am trying to hurry to get down the steps as fast as I could. Gunner is very personable. He was trained in Germany. He loves to bite. All I can think about as I am going down the steps is that one of the idiots in their fear of a police dog might kick him. Then he would go off on them! Yes, he likes to bite but he will not bother you until you bother him. When people ask if he bites, I always tell them all dogs bite! But he will not bite you unless I give the command. Turns out Gunner did not bite anyone—he was just visiting.

Saint Columbkille is our parish. They must be crazy, as they gave me the church for K-9 training. I hid dope all around the church. Then I did a demo for the little kids. It was a brand-new place, and Gunner found heroin in the pulpit!

Once we were in the home of a woman who was a mason. She was very good with her hands. Cleveland had called to let me know that a guy they'd arrested could tell me about some guy who would tell me where he got his dope. They had a search warrant for a house in the suburbs. They could not find anything, so I was called in. I got there about 2 a.m.—a very nice split-level home. I met the sergeant outside, and he told me there should be three ounces of cocaine inside someplace. That is a decent amount, but not great. I went upstairs with Gunner and then to the kitchen. Nothing. We went into the living room. Nothing.

Next we went into the family room. Gunner was off the lead. He began to run along the wall and he was going nuts. There was a couch on that wall. I moved the couch, trying to get him to pinpoint where he was alerting. He was getting frustrated. He was mainly getting upset at me for not understanding. He kept hitting on the wall. We get crowbars to pull off the paneling. Nothing. There were shelves. We tried pushing on them and suddenly there was a door! We had wrecked the paneling before we found the hidden door. We found five to six kilos of cocaine, submachine guns, money, and jewelry. This all belonged to the woman; it was all hers. That was one of the more unique finds we have had, along with the find in the toilet. I was very proud of this.

Gunner has found dope in someone's mouth, about a dozen rocks of crack in his mouth. The bad guy thinks, *I will not swallow it. I do not want to go to jail, so I will keep it in my mouth.* They simply do not think that it could kill them.

None of my dogs has been very aggressive. My first two were goldens; they did their job. They would scratch to alert. But Gunner thinks about it. The other two would just do it and get it over with and go on their merry way. If Gunner was searching a room, he would come in the door and stop. He would figure out where the odor was, if there was an odor to find. If it was hidden in a plant, for example, he would pass it, but I could tell he had found the dope because of how he would look at me. Still he would continue searching the whole room. He would keep looking for me. Why? I could not figure this out for the longest time. But soon as I would turn my back, he would be at the plant ripping it to shreds. He knew if I got there first I wouldn't let him rip it, so he tries to get to it before I can get to it! He really thinks about his plan.

A lot of times, we get a suspect package. We will put the box on the other side of the chain link, so Gunner cannot get to it. He will go by and pass it, but he knows that there is an opening further down, so if he goes past the package, he will look at the opening, so he can get to the box and rip it to shreds. He loves to rip and tear. He loves to play tug-of-war with the reward terry-cloth towel. Whenever I visit the fire station, they tell me their towels are disappearing. They are blaming me. I think that is very rude of them.

When we are going out on a marijuana bust, we do encounter booby traps. We have seen fishhooks hung to catch eyes, trip wires, and punji sticks. We have seen all sorts of things used to outsmart us. It is not just set up for law enforcement but for anyone who might want to take the growing marijuana plants. These guys try to protect their wares. I have learned to be careful in any entry. I don't care if it is a hotel room, a house, or a car. I have to make certain that we are protected, especially our animals. If we make an entry, the dog is not the first one in. The SWAT team will make entry and secure the residence, and only then do I bring in my dog. What I normally do is like painting the floor. I start at the further end; it could be the attic or basement. That depends on the house. I am the only one with a dog, and I do not want his attention diverted. Later a second dog could come in and that is OK.

Gunner found drugs in a basement. He was searching very well when I looked up in the rafters and saw a plastic bag! "Geez! Gunner you have been making me so proud of you, but you missed something. I can even see this." I got my finger and thumb on the bag, and as I pulled it off the rafter, the weight of it pulled it right out of my hand. It was a grenade! I yelled, "Grenade!" Everyone stopped. It just so happened we had an ATF (Alcohol, Tobacco, and Firearms) officer with us. He very calmly said, "Everyone out!" He had not finished the word *out* before we were all out of there. It doesn't take a Ph.D. to figure out this was not my kind of search. It is things like that that make my job interesting.

When we have a day off, Gunner goes nuts. He is fine for about six hours, but he wants to go to work. On those days, if I go out for any errand and leave him home, he gets very testy. All I do is drive him, I clean out his truck, I do his paperwork, I clean up his backyard, and I feed him. I make sure he has all of his shots, but other than that he does all the work.

I was taught those three words: *Trust your dog.* The human mentality is that we often think we are smarter than our dogs. When a new handler is trying to have his dog certified, he is very nervous. The dog is telling him right where the drugs are hidden, but the handler is often too nervous and keeps pointing out other places for the dog to check. He has not yet learned to trust his dog.

When we go out, we call it going fishing. Some of our best contacts are delivery truck drivers. One was complaining that he had three of the same suburban electronic stores on his route—but one always gets ten to fifteen boxes every Saturday. The other two stores do not get any deliveries on Saturdays. I looked at one of packages; the return is out of Pittsburgh. I ran the tracking that showed it was actually coming out of Southern California. Something is wrong. Just for giggles, we hide one of the containers and let my dog find it. The container had 30 pounds of marijuana. The total for all the boxes turned out to be about 250 pounds of marijuana.

This was a Saturday. I did not want to get someone out on his day off. So we did what I call bag and tag, keep the information and just hope we get lucky again. On Tuesday, I go back and see the same type of boxes coming in to the same mailing facility. I said to pull them off the line. We ended up with a repeat load with about 500 pounds of marijuana bound for the same suburban store. When the manager took possession of the packages, we arrested him. We did a search of the suspect's house. He had been ripping off that store of everything they sold. He is in prison right now. He lived right in that same town.

Just last week, a shipment of ecstasy tablets came from Budapest being shipped to Maple Heights. Drugs did not start yesterday; they started a long time ago. The educational system should have helped, but people are still going to experiment. That is reality.

I do not believe that just because someone is picked up for the first time they should be given probation. That is just my opinion. I do not want that person out on the street. A gram of narcotics can go for $100 to $150. That is why there are burglaries and thefts. People often hurt their own kind when they buy drugs. Any home can be broken into; even mine had been broken into before we moved here. There is nothing that can mask the odor of drugs for a dog except one thing. No air! Maybe inside a space suit? If any air can leak out of a drug package, the dog can find it. Nothing can mask it. Nothing.

I had the first specialty dog in the area. He was not aggressive, and he was not a patrol dog. He was trained to find narcotics. You name a police department, and I have worked with them. It has made me feel good that they saw the need for the dogs and wanted a working team in their department. It probably all started with BCI (Bureau Criminal Investigation) letting me get a dog and basically letting me go out and help other departments. A drug dog is not the total answer, but it is a way to go. My first dog was a border collie, Chaz. She was a very loving dog. I taught her to find marijuana. Red was my second dog and Gunner my third. He loves kids, women, and men in that order. I am blessed as one of the first in the area. I have had so much fun doing this. I would rather have a working dog for a partner then a human.

Detective Ed Roman

Cuyahoga County Sheriff's Office, Cleveland, Ohio
K-9 Doc

Ed told me many interesting facts about working with the narcotics unit, most of them simply ingenious but secret, so I cannot describe them. We were having a quick lunch before he was to give a demo to a senior citizen's group. I said I could not visualize a gram of anything, much less a narcotic. Ed picked up a sugar packet, ripped off one corner, and slowly poured the sugar in a line on the table. I wish you could have seen the waitress's face!

I have been involved in law enforcement for twenty years. I first became a full-time deputy with the narcotics unit involved with controlled purchases (drug buys) and search warrants. In 1995, I was asked to be a K-9 handler for a narcotics-sniffing dog. I agreed to the added responsibility if I could have a German shepherd. In the beginning, I spent two weeks with K-9 Doc, just playing with him and letting him get used to my wife and children. After a four-week training course, Doc and I were certified in narcotics detection. To continue our training, I met with a group of handlers from various local police departments. I met one of the trainers who came across as stern and to the point. I was brand-new to this.

Doc was to find drugs hidden in some vehicles. The handler/trainer had no emotion on his face as he walked around telling me to check this and that. He kept watching me, and I was thinking this guy is going be tough on me. But Doc and I got through it and found all the hidden narcotics. He then pulled me off to the side and asked, "Why are you so nervous?" I said, "Because you are scaring the hell out of me." He asked what I meant. I told him I have a brand-new dog and no experience and you are so serious and know all about this stuff and I don't. He laughed and told me he was there to help me. All the other handlers were there to help me. He said all of them had started out just like me. No different. He told me if I made a mistake, they would tell me, so I could correct it.

Those twice-a-month training days were learning experiences to make all of us successful on the streets. I continued to go and got to know that handler as a good friend who was helpful, knowledgeable, and a great guy.

My dog was trained just for narcotics; other handlers with narcotics-only dogs would leave the training sessions after completing the narcotics searches. I would always stay for the whole time. I would put on the bite suit and work with the guys. I knew the handler was impressed, as he mentioned it several times. I knew I could call him any time of the day or night for advice, like the times Doc was sick.

In 1997, our sheriff's office decided to have dual-purpose dogs (narcotics and patrol with apprehension, tracking, and building search training.) The sheriff said we were doing high-priority warrants on dangerous guys with drug counts and gun specs, with no patrol dogs available—so it was time we had them. All felony warrants in the county come to the sheriff's office where they are entered into LEADS (the law enforcement computer). We have two teams of warrant detectives who track down and arrest people with outstanding warrants. We also arrest people who have been arrested by local police on felony warrants when they do traffic stops. The police check the subject's driving information and vehicle information when they run the warrants through computers. The warrant officers will have a K-9 assigned to them. This has greatly enhanced officer safety; also it pretty much stopped the suspects from running away.

I was sent to Columbus to train with the Franklin County Sheriff's Office. We completed patrol training, bite work, tracking, and building searches. I was then assigned to the night warrant team. My job was to cover the back door with K-9 Doc on every house where we worked a warrant. In a nine-month period, I was assigned to this unit at least a dozen times. The suspect would exit the back door while detectives were entering the front door. They would see Doc and me. Doc would bark, and the suspects would stop dead in their tracks, and I would arrest them. When you are dealing with these types of guys with serious charges, they want to get away. Many of them are twenty-two to twenty-five years old. If I was by myself, they would look at me (I am forty-six) and take a shot at running. But with K-9 Doc, they know they cannot outrun him. That makes our job easier and safer.

One interesting incident happened when we went to serve a warrant in a suburb. The subject was really a bad actor. He was wanted on rape, gun charges, and felonious assault on a woman. We checked with the police; they had had numerous run-ins with the guy. He liked to fight it out with the police. We got to the house and knew he was inside hiding. He was probably armed and one you would not mess with. The detectives said I should bring in Doc to find the guy. We first searched the basement. I sent Doc and followed behind him with a detective, our guns out, flashlights in hand. Before sending Doc, I made the announcement, "Sheriff's office, come to the sound of my voice, or I will send in the dog." (Doc is barking as I say this). I make three announcements before sending him. I don't need to command Doc to search. He knows what he is looking for: a bad guy (based on practice). We check the basement; the guy is not there. We go up to the attic. We've gone about three steps (suspect could hear us coming) when all of a sudden we hear, "Don't send the dog. I am coming out." He comes out of the attic with hands in the air, and we arrest him. As he was taken to our car, I had to ask him, "Why did you give up?" He said, "Hey, man, I watch *Cops* on TV. I have seen what those dogs do!" Another time, I asked the same question of a suspect. His reply, "I will tell you something, man. I will take a bullet before I get bit."

You can argue with a policeman, you can even fight with a policeman, but you cannot argue with a dog. He will not listen to you. He just will go in and do his job. These guys know that once these dogs come looking for them, the dog will find them and they will get bit! It is the fear factor that promotes the officer's and the bad guy's safety. Arresting a subject without incident is our goal. I know what it is like to get bitten. When I was a paperboy, I was bitten by a collie and had seventeen stitches in my back. It was very frightening. A few times in training, I have been bitten. Nothing serious, but it hurts! It is a scary feeling when an animal bites, even if it is a squirrel. The fear factor really promotes safety when dealing with the bad guys.

My job with the sheriff's office is rather unique. I'm a narcotics officer and K-9 handler. In most police departments, an officer will get called to do a building search or narcotics searches. The detectives or police officers who call you complete the case and take it to the next level. When working with the warrant teams, if drugs are found, I handle the case when assigned to narcotics. I generate my own cases and assist my unit members with K-9 narcotics searches. I really enjoy my job. We are also involved in drug interdiction. We check places for incoming narcotics like the airport, trucking companies, bus stations, train stations, and mailing facilities. When assigned to interdiction, it's not just me; my partner also is a handler with K-9 Marli. There are a bunch of other guys from other agencies, like DEA, Customs, FBI, and other local departments.

When working mailing facilities, if we find a dope package, it's something that has to be well orchestrated in order to deliver it in a timely manner. We arrive at the facility at 6 a.m. and start checking packages. You would be surprised to see how fast they can unload and sort three thousand packages that are going down a belt.

By 8 a.m., the trucks are loaded and ready to roll. If we find a package at 7:55 a.m. we still have to stay just in case there could be a second one. There have been times when we have signed three or four dope packages. We have to run downtown, fight rush-hour traffic to get a search warrant for the package. After opening the parcel and inventorying the contents (narcotics), we have to check the address, get a description of the house, apartment, or business in order to get a search warrant for that location when delivery is made.

We have to coordinate the delivery and have enough manpower to hit the location, search it, and make arrests. These parcels have to be delivered by 11 a.m. or people will not accept them. This can be a logistical nightmare at times. My partner and I have it down to a science; we split the work and save a lot of time by writing our own warrants. The warrant wording is pretty routine; we just have to change some of the descriptions. We have delivered dope packages throughout the county and many suburbs.

I have worked parcel interdiction with another handler from an adjoining city; I call him the parcel guru. He has taught me how it is done; he is a great instructor, and I like to think I have been a good student.

There are so many neat aspects to this job, I never get bored. I do drug buys, search warrants, fugitive warrants, and interdiction duties. I love my job and I enjoy having a K-9 partner; it is extra work but very rewarding. I am just one of the guys who likes to be busy and in the midst of things. It is just fun. I hate to take a day off because I am afraid of what I will miss.

Tracking

Deputy Terry Fleck

El Dorado County Sheriff's Office, Placerville, California
K-9 Blazer

Terry was an instructor for a two-week training session in Florida. He would often drive me to the next training site. On the way, he would explain what I had just observed and what would be happening next. He was very popular with all the K-9 handlers. Some of them decided to play a joke. They filled a large plastic baggie with dog poop and secretly put it under the front seat of his car (the one I was sharing with him). As we left the site, I asked if he would like me to tell him something important now or later. Then I got his story.

On Saturday, February 6, 1993, a thirty-three-year-old man and his wife drove up to the South Lake Tahoe area to "play in the snow" for the day. Shortly after arriving at 10:45 a.m., the man's wife went back to the car, which was parked about fifty yards away. She got her jacket, but when she turned around her husband was gone.

The man suffered from a neurological disorder, which resulted in a memory disorder. He had made two prior suicide attempts. He was dressed in a cotton sweatshirt, cotton sweatpants, and tennis shoes. The weather was clear and cold, about forty degrees. His wife searched for him for two or three hours but did not locate him. Thinking he may be attempting suicide again she contacted 911. It was unknown if the man was armed.

Upon the first deputy's arrival, I was paged to respond with Police Service Dog K-9 Blazer to conduct a search for a missing suicidal man. Due to the possible suicide attempt, the first deputy had determined that this search should be a law enforcement response, not a search-and-rescue response. I arrived at 2:45 p.m. and began searching using Blazer as a locating tool.

Blazer was not only trained for aggressive search; he was also trained in search-and-rescue nonaggressive search. In nonaggressive search, he would locate the victim and then do a RECALL/FIND, which means he would come back to me, bark at me, and then direct me to the victim. I started this search with a nonaggressive SEARCH command, realizing I could change my dog's response into aggressive search if needed.

The man had a four-hour head start on us. If Blazer could determine a direction of travel, that would cut our search area in half. The search area was a large canyon area with a large river flowing through it. The snow was soft in the sunny areas allowing a person to posthole up to their waist in it. In the shaded areas, the snow was hard-packed ice, which did not show any type of visual tracking sign.

Blazer picked up a scent where the man was last seen. I also saw a visual sign of a tennis shoe type print. I believed we were tracking the man. The track immediately led to the American River in deep water. Blazer went across the river and I did as well. Blazer continued tracking to the west, downriver. I realized the victim could be wet in hypothermia-prone cotton, probably for hours. About a quarter of a mile later, Blazer crossed the river again. I did as well and saw a tennis shoe print on the riverbank heading west.

I directed the other deputies by radio of our direction of travel. I directed the deputies to spread out in half-mile intervals and then leapfrog into the search area. I was hoping the deputies would either cut the man off and locate him or see visual sign of him. If visual sign was located, then additional dog teams could be leapfrogged ahead to that new point last seen. I requested additional police service dog teams to respond to the search.

Blazer continued to work the scent. I occasionally saw other signs of the tennis shoe print. I would loose that sign on the hard-packed ice. The track started meandering as though the man was disorientated. I assumed the man was either disoriented or hypothermic or both. I lost any visual sign of the man and simply followed Blazer.

Meanwhile the other deputies were leapfrogging ahead of me. They had not located the victim or any visual sign. Blazer located two of the deputies. It was apparent that the man was still continuing west, already ahead of some of the deputies

About thirty minutes later, I saw a behavioral change in Blazer. His head came up off the track, his tail started wagging, and he took off at a run. I had lost sight of him but continued in that direction at a jog. About fifteen minutes later, I heard Blazer below and behind me. He came into me at a full run, stopped, and started barking at me. I commanded him to re-find the man. It took two RECALL/FINDS over about five minutes for Blazer to bring me to the man.

The sun had set and the temperature was about twenty degrees. The man had postholed in the snow up to his waist. He was wet head to toe, unconscious and unresponsive. I notified the other deputies of my location. Due to the leapfrogging, they had a good idea within a quarter of a mile where I was.

I pulled the man out of the snow and over to a tree well where it was dry. It appeared that he was in the third stage of hypothermia. I stripped off his wet clothing. I put my clothing, including my hot bullet-resistant vest, on the man. As an emergency medical technician, I have rewarmed numerous hypothermia victims. I have never seen a victim rewarm as rapidly as this man. I believe the heat captured in my bullet-resistant vest was the key factor in his rewarming.

The man regained consciousness and was stuporous. By now, the other deputies and medical personal arrived. They took over the care and transportation of the man. I praised Blazer for a job well done, feeding him dog cookies as a reward.

The physicians I spoke with at the hospital all agreed that the man would have died within thirty to sixty minutes had he not been discovered by Blazer. I attributed the victim's survival to the expeditious tracking by Blazer. There was no way the slow process of visual tracking, even if possible, would have gotten us to the victim in time. Other deputies had been leapfrogging behind the man. They had not seen his visual track. It was clearly Blazer's tracking that made the difference between life and death.

Blazer had made numerous finds, arrests, and discoveries during his career. This was the first time he had saved a person's life. The K-9 team—Blazer and I—was awarded the Bronze Medal of Valor by the El Dorado County Sheriff.

The incident was a great example of the use of a police service dog as a locating tool. Not only did Blazer locate the man; Blazer saved his life.

Of all the arrests, finds, and recoveries I have seen my three dogs do in twenty-two years of handling, this is the one I remember the most. This is truly the story of a police dog making a difference.

Chief Carson Sink

Astatula Police Department, Astatula, Florida

K-9 Dixi

The Astatula Police Department prides itself on being the first municipal agency in Lake County to have a K-9 officer. The department consists of four full-time officers. I was very impressed to meet the Chief of Police Carson Sink, who is the K-9 handler. That team of a chief and his police dog seemed to explode with energy as I watched them during a week of rigorous training. After hearing Chief Sink's story, a handler remarked, "This is a good story of male pride and especially a cop's pride."

I was working the night shift when I saw a car coming my way; it was making a strange noise as though it had a flat tire. When the driver saw me, he turned off the car lights and took off driving down the road. I tried to stop him, but he kept speeding up. He did have a flat tire, which came apart and began making sparks. He had turned off the headlights, driving in the dark with a trail of sparks shooting out. He got to a construction site and bailed out of the car. I saw there were two men. One was tall; the other was short. I knew the small one might be a juvenile, so I did not want to deploy my dog. I knew that they had done more than speeding when I yelled to them to stop. I lost sight of them.

I went back to their abandoned car and saw TVs, radios, and guns. I knew this was a burglary, so I called for more backup, including the helicopter. A perimeter was set up, and I began to track with my dog. Dixi is a female and exceptionally strong. As we were tracking, she kept stopping at hot spots, places where the two suspects had probably rested for a few minutes. The scent was very strong in those places. She continued to track and find hot spots closer together. I turned my flashlight on less and less, as I did not want them to see us. The tracking was in sand mines. Where the sand had been removed, there were lakes and pits. I had my K-9 Dixi on a thirty-foot lead; she was about twenty feet ahead of me. She jumped over some low bushes to the other side. There were actually two dirt roads running parallel with the bushes in between. I followed her through the bushes. All of a sudden, my whole world changed immediately. I had fallen into a hole at least twenty-five or thirty feet deep. My dog had been able to jump across the hole, but with my flashlight turned off, I simply did not see it.

I was in the hole; I was looking up at my dog looking down at me! I had my radio, but I was too embarrassed to call anyone to come get me out of the hole. The pilot in the helicopter kept calling me, asking where I was. But I did not want to answer, as I was too embarrassed. I tried to dig hand and foot holds, so I could climb out, but they quickly refilled with sand. I told my dog PLOTZ, which means "lay down." I still had her lead in my hand. I had not dropped it in my fall. She was attached to one end, and I was attached to the other end. I was able to climb out without pulling her into the hole.

I was so filthy.

Other officers who had been working the perimeter caught the suspects in a convenience store. They asked me what had happened. I said, "Nothing!"

Deputy Chris Stratton

Claremont County Sheriff's Office, Batavia, Ohio

K-9 BUFFY

I met Chris in the sheriff's office. I told him that I knew abso-
lutely nothing about bloodhounds. I enjoyed watching Chris's
face light up as he told me abut Buffy and his love of being a K-9
handler. Many of Buffy's antics had us both laughing.

My K-9 Buffy is a very friendly bloodhound. She is very good at what she does, but she has absolutely no obedience at all. I have had German shepherds as pets but did not know about bloodhounds. The day I got her, I took her out back and cut her loose. She took off running. I am chasing a dog I had just gotten! I lost forty pounds that year chasing Buffy.

Later I got a second bloodhound, a male. He jumped the kennel fence and the surrounding six-foot yard fence, and we never saw him again.

You cannot have a bloodhound in your house because they chew like a three-week-old puppy. They also dig. Mine have destroyed an air-conditioning unit and chewed all the couch cushions on the chairs by my pool as well as all the wicker lawn furniture.

Buffy is very vicious with other dogs. She thinks she is bigger than she is. Last summer while on a trail, two Saint Bernards attacked us. She thought she was tougher than they were. They tangled, and all three had to be maced to separate them. A bit of mace can be washed out; I did not want her injured.

Anyone who takes a bloodhound makes a major sacrifice; it is not all the glory like the German shepherds get. I do not take her on patrol, so she stays in her kennel until I get called out. I have a second male bloodhound; he drools and shakes the drool everywhere. Buffy does not drool. I keep them pretty lean through the summer, but in the winter I beef them up a bit because their kennel is outside. If I bring them inside, they pant and shed. I have three doghouses made of one-inch plywood with Styrofoam insulation. I do tie a mud flap on the door, but they tear it off. I have had to reshingle their houses three or four times because they ate the shingles.

When Buffy bloated the first time, the vet found wood chips inside her. She was eating the wood from her doghouse. She is very high-strung. But she has done me well. She is certified by the state of Ohio.

When we run a trail, she wears a harness that says SHERIFF on it. She only wears it when she is working. She knows when I put it on her that she is going to work. When she sees me putting on my boots, she begins to pace. It is always a fight to take one of them and leave the other one. They both want to work. If I take Buffy, the male will howl until she comes back. Buffy has been certified a Distinguished Expert by the North American Work Dog Association. She has been given the National Police Bloodhound Association's Lifesaving Award. We do train hard. Sheriff Rodenberg is very supportive.

Having a bloodhound is an expensive venture for a department. Some get a hound, then discontinue the program. To be a bloodhound handler takes a different type of person. You cannot be wishy-washy or prim and proper. Your dog will jump on you, leaving dog hair and dirt all over your uniform. You must be able to take the smell. Bloodhounds have an odor of their own; it is the oil in their skin. I can give them a bath, then a few hours later they smell the same. I clean their ears, but they still smell in a few days.

Buffy has been attacked in a bean field. The guy she had been tracking was choking her. He took her to the ground, but even then she would not bite him or defend herself. That is one of the limitations of a bloodhound in police work. Their only purpose is to track. We do not do cadaver work. She is actually afraid of dead people.

We had a case where an elderly man was deer hunting in the backwoods. The family called us when he did not return home. We used a piece of his clothing for Buffy to scent. We began a track into the woods. It was my dog's first encounter with a dead body. She became so frantic, I had to put her on a choke chain and walk her out of the woods.

The next body we had was also an elderly person. My dog stuck her nose into a well. She jumped backward, scared. Everyone said they had checked the well. I almost pulled her off but remembered to "trust your dog." Each time I have forgotten that, I've screwed up. I leaned over the well and saw a blanket and then a foot. Buffy was as scared as though a raccoon had hissed at her.

When I first started with a dog, I made a platform for the police car myself. I had to put it in my car each time I was called out and take it out later. I bought my own uniforms for trailing. Instructor Andy Rebmann gave me harnesses and leashes. I had no idea of what training was needed—none at all. At first, I would take off running behind her, running as fast as I could while holding onto her leash. Instructor Denny Guzlas quickly broke me of the running. Buffy has had a broken foot, probably from a rock while she was tracking. She has had stitches on most of her body. She has been through the wringer. She has been caught in an electrical cow fence that wrapped around her as she fell. She has been choked and maced and attacked by dogs.

Buffy is a small dog, only about sixty pounds. That is in her favor for going over fences when she is tracking. I do not want her to go over a fence unless someone is there to get her on the other side. I pick her up and hand her over. When I got her, I had no idea of what would be involved, absolutely none. I thought it would be all glory and fun. This is not the case! Since then many of my holidays have been spent training Buffy. When my pager goes off, I have had to leave my wife in restaurants or recitals and depend on her parents to get her and the kids home. I average about fifty to sixty call-outs a year, and my pager goes off at any hour of the day.

I don't know if I would ever have another female hound again. If I am having a bad day and raise my voice, it is all over. She will take off running in the wrong direction. She is a handful. She is a good worker with a lot of drive, but I would like to have her drive and heart in a dog with patience.

A bloodhound's ears droop down and make a cone that helps with the scenting. She does get slobber all over her ears. Her ears do get beat up a lot when her nose is dragging in the briars. She is able to both ground- and air-scent, using what works best to find the lost person. It is phenomenal how far she can scent. She would never bite to defend herself; she is so very gentle that there is never any fear of having her around children. I do demos every year with mentally challenged individuals. She lets them grab her tail or pull her ears. I never worry that she might hurt someone.

When she sees someone in a wheelchair, she will put her head in their lap. A very, very gentle dog.

We were called out to find a suicidal person. His mother told me he had just gotten out of the penitentiary. He was over six feet tall and 250 pounds. He was seen carrying a butcher knife. He had said he hates the police. Buffy is not the type of dog you want to track that type of person. But we were there and had backup guys with Tasers. As we got to the end of the track she became very excited; her tail was going a mile a minute as she jumped around. I was able to hold on to her. The officers turned on some lights, and there he was in the bushes just five feet from me, fortunately he gave himself up. But that is a dangerous situation, to have a bloodhound tracking an armed and violent person.

At times, the dogs can be more of a hindrance than a help. They are great in finding kids and Alzheimer's patients, especially as there is no fear these dogs would bite anyone. That works well in court. Another benefit is the way they can trail in a very contaminated area, even downtown. They can work a longer trail than other dogs.

A three-year-old boy had chased kittens into the woods. When I went to the creek bed, I could not pinpoint where he was. The water was moving. Over several hours, two hundred foot-searchers were assembled. The first team found the little boy alive even before the second team was assembled. That was a very rewarding search for us.

A mother in a mobile home park warmed up her car; she put her little one in the baby seat and went back into the house for something. As she came outside, she saw a man running, carrying her child. We went three-fourths of a mile into a field where we saw the guy running. He was holding the baby like a football. We got him! As with other cases, once we find the lost person my job is over. I do not always know what happens to the bad guys.

We have worked with the FBI on bank robberies. Definitely different. In Reading, Ohio, the robber dropped the money with the dye pack. That was the beginning of our track. It is very hard to go through shopping centers and towns. People would come out and want to pet Buffy. I had to tell them we were working and could not stop. My backup is very important. I take as many as I can get. Once I had a whole SWAT team in pursuit with me.

A man robbed a store and began to drive down the wrong way on I-275. He shot up a police car, then ditched his car and ran. He has a towel wrapped around his head. When the towel dropped of, that gave Buffy the scent article. She tracked him through the mall and up to a doorway where he had been seen. There was a video surveillance tape of him. We may not always find the guy, but if we can find a lead or evidence to help close a case, that is part of her job also.

We find guys who run from domestic violence. They beat up their partners and take off. A lot of our tracks are rural. We have faced a lot of suicidal subjects. We found one man out in the pasture. He was so scared of Buffy that he just laid down, dropping his knife. He was sure she was vicious. I played into that. She moved so quickly to find him that I found myself without a backup able to keep up with us. I have four legs pulling me over hard pavement. I have to keep very fit just to keep up with her. She pulls me very hard. I have found myself more than once out in the woods with only my dog. I am suddenly face-to-face with a guy with a knife. I only have a dog!

Once a guy we were trailing got to a golf course and stole a cart. His scent was falling off the cart. We found the cart by the fairways where he had set fire to it. It was interesting that Buffy had been able to follow the scent from a moving golf cart. We did not find him. That was something I had to get used to. People who commit crimes often have a getaway car waiting for them.

It took me two years to find out what had actually happened at a bank robbery. The husband-and-wife team had earpieces and microphones. When he was running and saw police, he would call her to set up another place for the getaway. I always want to know the ending, good or bad.

Once I was chasing a bad guy. Later when I interviewed him in jail, he told me that some guy was chasing him with a big brown dog coming right at him. He lay perfectly still, so the man stopped and put the dog up. The guy had only been fifty yards ahead of me, but I was being a bonehead by not trusting Buffy. I had blown it. I told the guy, "That was me." He said if he had known that he would have come out. We were that close. One of my trainers had told me that if Buffy and I ever messed up it would be 90 percent handler error. He was very blunt with me, but he was so right. Every time I have messed up, it was my fault.

Some boys broke into a Subway store by throwing a rock through the window. They took money from the cash register. Officers on patrol found a group of boys playing basketball past curfew. They denied robbing the store. No suspects and no leads. I scented Buffy on the rock found in the store. She took off running to the boys, jumping up on one of them. He yelled, "What is that dog doing?" We took him back to his house, where he confessed. Buffy had his scent from that rock!

There were a string of pharmacy burglaries. OxyContin and methadone were stolen. We were going down behind businesses in the pitch-black dark when Buffy stopped and jumped up on a police car. She began scratching at the car door, I told her to get down. I could see a cop inside writing his reports. I tried to get her to move along, but she would not. I did not know there was a guy in the backseat of that patrol car. She was trying to tell me that he was the burglar, but she couldn't talk. Buffy had found him in the police car. He finally confessed.

An arsonist burned down a school. Buffy and I began at the site and took off through a large crowd of people. Again she jumped on a police car. There was a guy inside writing a statement. He had called in the fire. He confessed that night that he was the one who set the fire. He had then walked to a phone booth to call it in: "I was just walking by when I saw the fire." Buffy solved that one, too. Without her, we might not have closed that case.

A bloodhound's training is started on puppy trails. Another officer or trainer will tease them with food and a scent article, and then give them a command. The only command Buffy knows is FIND 'EM. I say it one time only and that is enough. The trainer runs off, and I let her go after him. There is a lot of screaming and yelling. When the hounds find the "lost person," they get a lot of praise. That is done over and over. I used to train her three to five times a week when I was single. I was very dedicated.

I testified in a pizza man robbery. The pizza man would be delivering a pizza in a mobile park home. A guy would jump out with a knife taking both the pizza and the money. We began the trail inside the mobile home to eliminate what we call the "missing man" theory. The theory is if three of us are here and one of us leaves, the dog is brought in to smell the odor of the two people. There is a scent missing. That is the missing scent she will look for. We went through the entire park. There were cats and trash everywhere. Our trail ended on a porch of one of the homes. No one was home. I cast her around giving her a chance to go in a different direction. She went to a truck beside the house. Inside the truck was a pizza box. We canvassed the area and went across the street. The occupants of that mobile home had gone across the street to use the pay phone for the pizza. We did not physically grab them but took the detectives to the spot where they found the man. He later confessed.

More on the "missing man" theory. Andy Rebmann at a seminar had identical twins who always ate the same foods and used the same laundry soap. How could a bloodhound locate the correct scent? The twins' mother gave Andy two socks, labeled sock one and sock two. The dog picked the right girl for the right sock. If I had not seen that, I would not have believed it. There is always a scent. That is the easy way to sum up every single crime scene; there is always evidence there. I have had Buffy put her nose on door handles at robberies and on countertops in a bank. The FBI had the robbery note, but I could not use it. She could leave her slobber or hair on the note. I had to put her on the countertop where the robber had leaned, and she could use that.

At one bank robbery, we found the presidential mask the robber had used. If I can get to an area to knock on doors, I might find someone who would say, "I saw a black car with Kentucky plates." All leads help and may mean a success, in my opinion. Going out into the woods to trail a person is great, but those situations are few and far between when I am working a case that is two days old.

In a residential area, we were looking for a sawed-off shotgun that was used in a double homicide. That was a big concern for the police as it was somewhere in the neighborhood. Buffy does not sit for her alerts. She has a slight change in her behavior. I feel I know her pretty well. When she first paused, I thought she was screwing around. I wanted her to get to work, as this was a very serious case. There was a privacy tree line separating the houses. Buffy would jump in and come out and then repeat that. I knew a lot of people were watching. I told her she was embarrassing me. She finally got out of the scent pool where the bad guy had bedded down to hide from us. Buffy continued the same pace the rest of the day. I decided we needed to go back to check that location. We went, and there it was! I had her on a thirty-three-foot lead that day, so she was a long way in front of me. If not, I probably would have seen the shotgun the first time. That had been the only place her behavior changed. She did not stop, but she kept going to the same area. In a couple of miles, she had only stopped once. There it was! There was a fingerprint on the gun that led to a conviction for a double homicide.

I used to put an article in a plastic bag for her to scent. Now, as soon as I pull out a plastic bag, she gets crazy. If I pick up her leash and put on my boots, she can tell the difference in my clothes and knows we are going to work. When I have on my coveralls and ball cap, she is all fire, running around. Once she was so excited, she fell into my pool. She had forgotten there was a large hole in the ground. She is very single-purposed. Very driven.

I met a whole group of patrol dog handlers in Kentucky. They were all very macho. They had not seen a bloodhound work. They thought I had a floppy-eared dog that didn't bite. What good could my dog be? What is she used for? I was standing over her with my Baggie and she was all fired up. I had her on a fifty-foot leash, she blasts off, and I missed the end of the leash! I was running behind her, chasing my own dog. That was an icebreaker, all the other handlers were laughing. I did not catch her. I was screaming to the guy at the end, "Get the leash." I knew she could just keep running and not come back. She would run until she was tired, then I could come to get her. I never take her off leash. Never, ever. Fortunately, that day she stayed on trail, and the guy at the end who had the hot dog treat was able to grab her leash.

She used to jump the fence at her kennel and go to one of the patrol dog handler's homes, two houses behind mine. He would call me to come get her. She is a very food-driven dog. I can walk her without a leash if I have a bowl of food—she will stay with me. To get her into the kennel, I would hold up my hand and toss in a treat. She would bolt right inside. Now I only have to hold up my hand and in she goes. She could care less about a ball except to chew it up.

An eighty-eight-year-old man with mental and medical problems had walked off. The K-9 unit in his county had been looking for him in the wooded areas. I scented Buffy with a pair of pants given to me by the family. Many had searched, yet Buffy was able to pick up his trail six-and-a-half hours later. She found him facedown, but alive. It was amazing. The family was thrilled.

I was called to the penitentiary in Ross, Ohio, to assist in finding an escaped prisoner. The officers there had drug dogs only. I ended up tracking to a Walmart where there was video surveillance. The escapee's clothes were found in the bathroom. He hid in the woods overnight and came back to the store in the morning to wash up and get some food. Prison officials found him in the store. I got a very nice letter from the state of Ohio.

A juvenile boy had been missing for fourteen hours. His family and friends had searched the park for him. This contaminated the area, leaving many scents. This is where a bloodhound is so useful. They can scent-discriminate. I was called out. The boy's dad gave me a piece of his son's clothing. There were people everywhere. My sergeant kept everyone there. We took Buffy to each person, so she could scent them. In theory, since they were there, my dog should be not be looking for them. She smelled the boy's clothing and took off. I ran behind her with my backup unit. Some ninety minutes later, we found the boy. He was naked under a bush. He was a severe diabetic and in shock. We found the clothing he had discarded along the way. Buffy ran right past them. My backup team collected them. Buffy became very excited when she found the boy. He had taken some LSD, so there were a number of things working against him. The doctor told us the boy could not have made it much longer without insulin. That was my very best case. His mother came to the emergency room and hugged me. That find was very rewarding. I got the National Lifesaving Award for it. It was such a good feeling to know we had found the boy in time.

Sergeant Eduardo Jany

Monroe Police Department, Monroe, Washington
K-9s JAKE AND CHICO

Ed is a very charismatic K-9 instructor. He kept the men laughing as he told jokes in many different dialects, but first nodding to me to move out of hearing range. One of the training exercises was a car takedown. It was decided I could participate by being in the passenger seat of the "suspect's" car. I knew the whole scenario as they had gone through it verbally several times. But the element of surprise overwhelmed me when suddenly many officers with drawn guns materialized by my car window. It was a frightening moment. I cannot imagine what a bad guy must feel at such a moment. One of the officers yelled, "Look, it's Driving Miss Daisy," *referring to my age and the movie.*

I was born in São Paulo, Brazil. As a child, I spent a lot of time at my uncle's farm. Near there was a monastery where they raised German shepherds. There were several at our farm, and I loved to play with them, crawling in their kennels and running around with them.

I started as a foot patrol officer in housing projects in Minneapolis while in college at the University of Minnesota. I moved to Orlando and attended K-9 school with K-9 Jake in 1990. I came to Monroe in 1994 and started the K-9 program there with Jake.

A narcotics call came late at night. The task force officers stopped a car they had been doing a drug transaction with, and they were ready to arrest the suspects who had stashed the dope. After nearly ripping the car apart and taking apart even the engine pieces, they were puzzled and ready to give up. They knew these guys had a large amount of cocaine in the vehicle. I responded, put Jake in the car, and got a strong hit on the dashboard after less then thirty seconds' work. We pulled the panel and found two socks filled with coke.

One night, an officer and I were in the process of arresting and also in a fight with a rather large biker type. K-9 Jake recognized the struggle. He leaped from the car and took hold of the guy's leg, pulling him and rendering enough pain to allow us to get control of the guy's hands and arrest him.

In another case, I had only recently begun training on evidence. We were called upon to try to locate a gun buried near a schoolyard. It had been stolen during a burglary and was hidden in preparation for a robbery by some serious juvenile offenders. After a brief cursory search, I began to get an indication in some bushes. Minutes later, there is Jake digging next to an office building, pulling the butt of the gun out with his teeth.

Jake started out as pretty wimpy, not a strong dog, but very happy to work. He was more interested in drug detection and play then in bite work. I worked with the play, and as he matured he became very dynamic, agile, and fast. He made several high-profile apprehensions; one was a guy with three strikes against him. This guy had been breaking into homes to molest women as they slept beside their husbands. Jake was able to get a good track on him, stopped him with a bite to the stomach. Nice! Now the guy is in prison forever. Jake made so many apprehensions that the town named a street after him. Jake Drive! He was the Grand Marshall in the State Fair Parade.

One of the toughest things I've ever had to do was to put Jake down. He was suffering from a severe infection that caused constant pain to his ears and affected his brain. As a recon marine and a SWAT officer, I am accustomed to being somewhat callous, removed at times. But this affected me unlike anything I have ever had to deal with. It was so sad to see my best friend, my partner I had worked with for over ten years, slipping away forever. I had him cremated; his ashes are in a box with an engraved badge on it sitting under a drawing of him on my mantle.

Chico is my current dog. He also has made many high-profile cases. In one case, an individual had killed his own father and shot at a SWAT officer during a standoff. He was arrested. But years later, he violated parole and fled from an officer. He was considered a high-risk prisoner. The schools in the area were locked down; people were in fear. We began a track. After five hours and forty minutes Chico pulled me into a swamp. He swam ahead of me. I lost sight of him and heard yelling. He had literally swum underwater and grabbed the suspect by the shoulder. The suspect had been hiding partially submerged.

Although I love catching bad guys, I have one case that got me more emotional than any other. Chico and I responded to a missing three-year-old. The boy had walked away from his house in a rural area in East Snohomish County, Washington. The area is very hilly, forested. There are frequent bear and cougar sightings. It was nearly dark and the family was quite worried; they had searched for nearly thirty minutes with neighbors. We, too, searched for another hour. Search-and-rescue teams and helicopters were being called to the scene. Chico was taking me all over, something not unusual with missing children; they tend to amble about to all sorts of interesting places. Suddenly—there he was! A cute, scared, crying three-year-old lost in a tall pasture clearing near the forest area. The boy got right up in my arms, and as we walked back to his parents, I had tears in my eyes. I was so proud of Chico, my partner, and so happy for the family. We now have about five child finds under our belt.

Chico remains a hit. Many times when I'm driving my patrol car, the kids will yell his name. As my department often reminds me, I am just the dummy at the end of the leash. Our chief once mentioned that I would be out of a job if Chico learns to drive. He was promoted to Master Patrol Officer. I am fortunate to have an agency that supports K-9 work and recognizes our successes.

I got involved in a shooting. I was shot and my dog was slightly injured. It was a total melee in a confined space. I lost a large chunk of my left forearm (about a third of my arm) and my ring finger. A .223 round ripped through my arm and took off the whole top of my arm. I have seen worse. I was able to go back to work in eight weeks. I have been very blessed; I cannot say it any other way. I have had a stellar K-9 career. I have very good stats and a great dog. I can turn him off and on. The beauty of this is he will go out to find the bad guy, get the bite, and I can call him off.

Later at home, he plays like a little kid, and I trust him with my young daughter. I do bring him to the office; there the worst thing he will do is to try to steal someone's food. He is still a dog, but a wonderful partner. Chico will probably retire next year at age ten. He is still agile, but our terrain is very mountainous. If we have a long track, it takes it out of him. If we track at night and it is cold, he is pretty well spent. I want him to have a good retirement.

I love training handlers. Many guys join K-9 thinking it will be a sexy job to be in. They wear a cool uniform. They could catch bad guys. They think the girls will be impressed. Bottom line is that if you don't just love being a handler, this can be the stinkiest job in the department. There is constant cleaning up poop and vomit, and fur everywhere. There are always extra reports. You have to love your dog. I do. You need passion for the job.

I am a lieutenant colonel in the U.S. Marine Corps on active duty in Brazil. Chico will live with me here until my assignment is over. I just completed a combat tour, now assigned to the U.S. Embassy, Brasília, Brazil, where I am working on counter-narcotics-counterterrorism ops.

Semper Fidelis! De Oppresso Liber!

Officer Jennifer McLain

Tequesta Police Department, Tequesta, Florida

K-9s HASSO AND MAGNUM

Jennifer is in southern Florida hurricane country. She worked 113 hours overtime during Hurricane Frances. She did a few short training tracks with her dog during a lull in the storm. Even when the wind was blowing so hard they had to brace against it, he kept his nose down and followed the track. Later, safely in his cage, he slept as the winds outside were 105 mph.

My K-9 partner, Hasso, and I were at tracking training. The tracks were in a twenty-five-acre lot overgrown with thigh-high grass, many trees, cactus, and the occasional rotting barbed-wire fence. The game plan was to take turns making a track for a K-9 team, then to double back and walk the track with them to ensure the team was working it correctly. We were working tracks with scent articles left on the track. I had a bucket full of scent articles that I had been handling over and over to cover them with my scent. A deputy approached us and said it was our turn to track. I handed him the bucket of twenty-five articles that ranged from items as small as an elastic hair band to a pair of sunglasses. I told the deputy to pick any five of the items. He was going to put them on the track as he went along.

The deputy disappeared into the bushes to start the track. A half hour went by and he still had not returned. It was getting dark; the trainers were beginning to worry. They thought about sending the helicopter to search for him. K-9 Hasso was a new dog that had never been trained to track in the dark. Finally, to our great relief, the deputy came back, he had gotten lost! He laughed as he handed the empty bucket to me. He asked if I had heard of Hansel and Gretel. He had used the scent articles as he laid the track, so he could find his way back. The trainers said we could call off the track as it dark and we were not trained in night tracking. I said I wanted to give it a try. I put Hasso's tracking harness on, grabbed a flashlight, and dragged the reluctant deputy back to beginning of the track.

My dog began the track very well. The tired deputy trudged along behind us with the empty bucket. Yahoo! We found the first article; Hasso was working correctly. Then we found the second one! My dog and I were really working as a team. As we rounded a corner, the deputy told me it did not look familiar. My heart sinks. Did we take a wrong turn? Where did we lose the track? Hasso was still leaning into his harness and working hard. I looked at the deputy and told him, "Follow me; I trust my dog." We kept going and now a barbed-wire fence is in front of us. My dog went to the fence and lay down. He had found one of the scent articles! GOOD BOY! I picked up a small green hair scrunchie from the grass. The deputy now had a huge smile. We maneuvered through the fence and resumed the track. Twenty yards later, the deputy told me he did not lay the track this way. Again I wondered if my dog could track at night. But Hasso was still working hard and seemed sure of what he was scenting. I again trusted him. This happened several more times, the deputy and I having the same conversations. But now I am sure I know I can trust my dog. We skimmed past the cactus, the bushes, in and out of the barbed-wire fences and down a sandy slope that made him snort a lot. We ended the track finding twenty-three out of the twenty-five items! That was more than I had hoped for. Even the deputy who was a seasoned K-9 trainer was excited how well Hasso and I did. That track will always be a strong memory for me. It was the basis for bonding between my dog and me.

I also am training a search-and-rescue dog, K-9 Magnum. He is my own personal dog. I took him to a police dog training seminar. Up to this point, I had done all of his training by myself and was looking forward to the challenge of this training. There were thirty-seven dogs from various agencies, including two from the Secret Service.

One evening, we went to a tire repair shop to do building searches. Each handler entered the building with his canine and one trainer. An officer in a bite suit (he is called a decoy) was hidden within the building, it was the job of the K-9 team to locate him. Because Magnum is used for search and rescue, he would not be biting the decoy. We were placed at the end of the rotation.

Magnum, the trainer, and I entered the building front door. Straight ahead was a service counter. I directed Magnum by giving him the command to SEARCH. I then reinforced the command with a wave of my arm in the direction I wanted him to search. Without hesitation, he moved off to check behind the service counter. Nobody there. We moved to the various offices. Each time, he would wait for my commands. They were all empty. We moved into the warehouse, and I directed Magnum to check down the different aisles. Still nobody. I called him to HEEL and proceeded down another aisle. The trainer was still behind us observing.

Occasionally, I heard a "good" or "OK," but not much more was said. We headed for the third aisle. It was a long one with a ladder at the end leading up into the loft. The warehouse was dimly lit, and I could hear Magnum taking deep breaths and making small snorts as he worked his way in and out of the stacks of tires. He reached the ladder, sniffed at the base of it, and began to climb it. I was watching him so intently that I jumped when the trainer exclaimed, "Good, tell him GOOD BOY. No, do not let him climb the ladder. We will never get him down!"

During the excitement, Magnum had begun to climb the ladder when I gave him the command. He looked at me and jumped off the ladder twisting his body in midair. As soon as his feet hit the ground, he was at a full run toward me. He tried to skid to a stop in front of me while he was in a sitting position. The floor was slippery, so all ninety-seven pounds of him slammed into me, knocking me into the trainer. We were doing our best not to fall backward onto the cement floor. We regained our composure and moved to the next aisle.

There was a stack of tires lying on its side forming a tunnel. I could hear his wagging tail beating the tires, *thump, thump, thump.* The trainer and I laughed. Nothing bothered this dog. He circled the floor several times like a dog looking for a place to nap. Then he started climbing the walls. I was bewildered by his bizarre behavior. The trainer told me to tell him GOOD DOG! The decoy was in the loft above that corner.

I was so proud of Magnum. I told him so as I hugged and petted him. He was a happy dog. The trainer told me that only three of the thirty-seven dogs had tried to climb the ladder and/or the walls to get to the decoy. Magnum was one of the three. When I got outside, I listened to my trainer bragging to other trainers and officers about Magnum's performance as if Magnum were his own dog. I was on cloud nine.

Lieutenant Tom McCaffrey

Geauga County Sheriff's Office, Chardon, Ohio
K-9s BANDIT, SHEBA, AND BRUTUS

It is easy to find Mac—just listen for his hearty laugh. This Irish lieutenant simply enjoys life. He and I gave a demo at Dentzler School in Parma to six hundred very attentive children. Mac was talking to the children before introducing Brutus when the children began to giggle. He looked behind him to see Brutus sitting beside me, licking my face! One time, I accompanied Mac to the women's jail at the sheriff's office. I felt sad to see the women reaching their arms through the prison bars as they tried to pet Brutus.

I am the first police officer in my family. As a kid, I always wanted to be an officer or an airplane pilot. It was hard to become a cop. When I first became a cop, I didn't tell my mom. I took the test and got interviewed. When I told her she said, "Oh my God, Tom. You are going to get yourself killed!" Well, I haven't done that. I have had thirty years and I want to stay on because I like it. I always liked dogs. I researched and presented the K-9 program to Sheriff James C. Todd. Bandit was my first K-9, and we were the first K-9 team in Geauga County.

In my tenure as a deputy sheriff, I have found many self-proclaimed experts who try to let me know the proper way to perform, and who try to correct my alleged flawed performance in training my K-9, or raising my child, or properly doing my job. When I receive these suggestions, I do not argue. I just nod my head and smile. After a K-9 demonstration at a fair, a lady began advising me on how to properly train my dog. She then asked me what type of dog Brutus was. Being stunned by this brainless question, I replied, "German shepherd." This lady replied, "Oh, I used to breed them." Must I say more?

Geauga used to have miles of cornfields, in some places you can still see the cornstalks. Now there seem to be buildings everywhere. There are still many Amish farms. They have their own schools. Children walk to school carrying their lunch buckets as they did in the 1800s. The schools are heated by wood. There are outhouses, one for the boys and another for the girls. All grades are in the same one-room schoolhouse. There are many small schools here because the children need to walk to school.

I do assist the DARE (Drug Abuse Resistance Education) instructors with appearances in Amish schools with Brutus. Some say the DARE program does not work. I see it as a good public relations tool. I always show the children drug training and the dangers that narcotics have on the abusers. An Amish school has about forty students, a mixture of first to eighth grades. Amish children rarely go past the eighth grade. They quit school and get a job. They are very silent children, rarely asking questions. They do have dogs as pets, but never allow a dog into their home. Amish teens do have a problem with alcohol and drugs. They continuously have a party every Sunday night. We have a problem with buggies being involved in serious accidents. In Geauga, the buggies must have lights after dark. If not, I will give a ticket. Other counties have different rules. Our roads are very hilly; many cars drive fast and do not see a buggy until they come upon it over the crest of a hill.

One time, Bandit and I were tracking down a couple of Amish children through a pasture. It was Halloween, and the teens were sneaking up to Amish farms in the dark to grab a buggy and place it on a roof. The buggies are very light and easily damaged. Suddenly, a cow started chasing Bandit. Those cows looked huge, so I ran like crazy and threw Bandit over a fence. Now the cows were coming after me. I tried to get over the barbed wire, but my shirt got caught and ripped right off. The deputies were laughing so hard, but I did get over the fence and outsprinted the cowherd. My bulletproof vest saved me from getting hurt by the barbed wire.

Another time, two males and a female were fleeing after breaking into a business. As they tried to get away, they wrecked their car. A deputy caught the female, but the males took off. My phone rang at 4 a.m. I was asked to bring Sheba to track the males. Most guys brag about their dogs alerting to drugs, but I am a people finder. That is what I like to do most. Sheba can track without a harness or lead. I let her go and she works it. If she gets too far ahead, I quietly whistle, so she will wait for me to catch up.

On this day she tracked for three or four miles. My command to pump her up is: DO YOU WANT TO TRACK? DO YOU WANT TO TRACK? I had a backup with me. It was a very hot day. We were tracking through cornfields and underbrush before finally coming to a clearing. As we came over a rise, I could see two heads far away. I told my backup to duck down. I got on my radio to try to secure the perimeter. They asked where I was. As if I would know where I was! All the woods looked the same. I saw the tall metal towers of the Middlefield Swiss Cheese plant in the distance. This helped, and I tried to estimate my location by the towers. I tried to get a new perimeter set up.

Then I started to track again. My backup was so excited. He started to jog, getting ahead of Sheba. I yelled at him to get behind my dog. Sheba made an immediate right turn into the brush. I ran with her and there were the two guys! The look on their faces when they suddenly saw two cops and a dog come out of the brush was marvelous. I told them not to run or my dog would bite them. We handcuffed them and then had to haul them back down the three or four miles in that heat. "Good track, Sheba! Good dog."

My land has a pond and a large wooded area in the back. My young son, Marty, was helping me cut firewood. He wandered a bit too far and the following is his story.

Marty McCaffrey, age five: "I got lost. I looked in the woods and then I could not find my way home. I began to panic. I yelled for help. I just stood there. Lots and lots of trees. I could not see dad. He had to send Brutus to find me. I heard Brutus coming. I was happy. Brutus licked me. He smells stuff. He found me."

Marty is a real character. When I do demos with Brutus, Marty often goes with us. He passes out small deputy sheriff badges for the children. Sometimes Marty plays pool with the trustees. At the end of the game, he will say, "Bye-bye, bad guys!" In our jail, a trustee is a misdemeanant who is trusted to do such jobs as cleaning our offices, shoveling snow, washing, and waxing the cruisers. It is a privilege to be a trustee; prisoners apply for the positions.

I seem like a nice guy, but I am Irish, you know what that means. When someone crosses the line, I was taught to push him back. We get kids stealing beer. They go into a convenience store, beat up a clerk, and take off. We had to call an ambulance for a clerk one time. The kids took off. They got into a big wreck as they were fleeing the convenience store. Their car went up an embankment about ten feet and into a tree. They were cut up and bloody.

I was one of the first cars there. I saw one kid mouthing off, blood all over him. I try to be nice to him and ask him to calm down, but he is calling me every name in the book and will not listen to me. I told him he did not understand. I am the guy you can talk to, and you are in a lot of trouble kid, you just don't know it. You aren't going to be mouthing off to me and get out of it. It boils down to the kid being a jerk. I told him he was way out of line. I placed him under arrest.

Now I have to find his buddy who took off. Brutus tracked about 150 yards in a wet, wooded area. I remember Brutus pulling very hard. His pulling made it hard for me to maneuver through the heavy vegetation. We finally found the fleeing person trying to hide behind a very skinny tree. Brutus did his normal intimidating audible utterances. I stated to this person if he started to run I would let the dog go. He did not move, and my backup handcuffed and frisked the suspect. As soon as he was handcuffed, his demeanor changed where he challenged both me and my dog with comments on how he could kill us. We had to take him screaming and calling us names. I kept thinking what would have happened to me if I had done what those kids did and my parents had found out.

Actually, their parents called the sheriff's office to complain. They were from Pennsylvania. There they have state police, the main law enforcement agency. In Ohio, we have the highway patrol. States differ with their law enforcement. The highway patrol has jurisdiction on public roads and state property. They cannot make arrests anywhere else. In Ohio, the sheriffs can make arrests statewide. The position of sheriff started in Ohio in 1788, making it the oldest law enforcement position in the United States.

People from Pennsylvania do not think I have any power at all. Many times on the freeway, a Pennsylvania car will pass my marked cruiser doing 80 mph in a 55 mph zone. The kids who hit the convenience store were booked and charged with strong-armed robbery. The parent could not believe the charges. That was the most exciting call of that day.

An eighteen-year-old kid was being brought to court but he escaped from the deputy. He had stolen a township truck filled with geraniums for the veterans' graves. He had been fleeing for three days. I was still asleep when the town of Chardon got a pursuit call. The kid wrecked the truck right by a railroad track. I was called out. I did not take time to put on my uniform but grabbed some clothes and called Sheba. I was just beginning to work her. She was my second dog. She was very hesitant about biting as she was new, but she was an excellent tracker. When I am called to begin a track, I have to know where to start.

Being the handler, I have to figure it out. In a big area with the next road two miles down, where should I begin? I am sure he isn't going to walk through brush. He will probably take the area of least resistance. So I went up on the railroad tracks. The sheriff came by in his Jeep to tell me the guy had been spotted up by a trailer park. He asked me to drive. I used to drive a Jeep up in the mountains. There were wetlands there, so the train tracks are built straight up forty feet. Jeeps are tippy. Hang on, Sheriff! I have my dog in the back, and off we go through the brush and come to the trailer park.

There are other handlers and dogs already there. We begin staging all the K-9s in different areas. I was the last one to arrive, so I got to begin in the junkyard. Nobody could catch this guy. They had been chasing him for three days. I started walking through the junkyard, and about three-fourths of the way Sheba starts alerting to a van with no tires. I looked in the van window and saw the guy in the back trying to get out the back door. In the meantime, the deputy has the airplane from the state patrol flying over and he is trying to talk to them. So I couldn't get onto the radio. I told the guy in the van, "Listen, if you get out the back door, I cannot catch you, but my dog can catch you and will bite you." The guy started to approach me. I knew I was stronger then he was, but he could outrun me. I got my hands on him; but I didn't have my handcuffs, so I dragged him out of the van and sat on him. Sheba ran over and began to lick his face. The guy, not seeing a uniform, kept saying, "You ain't no cop." The plane sees me and begins to circle; the deputy is still talking. He wouldn't get off the radio, so I couldn't let anyone know I had the guy. I was sitting on him. When I finally got through, they asked where I was. "Well, I am in the junkyard. I am underneath the plane." That was a funny one. They came to get the guy.

Sergeant Johnson always teased Bandit. Bandit always restrained from biting Johnson. Johnson would grab him by the muzzle and shake it. This happened several times. One day, the sergeant put his uniform hat on the briefing table as he relaxed. Bandit had his chance for revenge; he walked over to the table, took the Smokey the Bear-type hat, put it on the ground, and peed in it.

One time I had to correct Bandit, and he did not like that. I placed him in the cruiser. Later when I was on patrol I felt something warm on my neck and shoulders. Bandit had peed on me, expressing his opinion, and then ran to the back of the van where I could not reach his butt. I did discipline him.

An Ohio State Patrol officer was chasing a stolen car with two males. The car wrecked and the suspects fled on foot. It was a very cold night, snowing lightly but not sticking on the ground yet. Sheba was tracking. My backup could not keep up with me. I found the first suspect about three-fourths of a mile into the woods. I found a sturdy tree and handcuffed the suspect to the tree. I reported this over my radio, so someone could retrieve him. I then continued to track the second suspect, who ran into the other officers guarding the perimeter. They placed him under arrest. I was then advised that the first suspect could not be located! I went back into the woods to return to my cruiser. I was looking and calling the suspect who was somewhere still handcuffed to a tree. I was unable to find him. We organized a search party and finally found him. His main complaint was that he was very cold.

Another time, a suspect was running from me. He ran into the wooded area. I yelled to him, "I hope you have boots because there are snakes in there!" He ran right back out. I had never seen a snake there. Sometimes it is better to use your wit than to use your dog.

I was driving down a road while on midnight shift. I saw a parked van. I knew the city of Akron owned all the property, so I blocked the van and walked up to the door. I asked the man inside what he was doing there. He told me he was reading (it was pitch-black). I asked if he was an owl. I asked for his driver's license and ordered him out of the van. He wouldn't get out. I told him he was parked next to a junkyard, he could have stolen something, and that gives me the right to look through his van.

"Get out! If you do not get out, I will have to arrest you for obstructing justice. What do you want me to do, just walk away?" He told me I wasn't going to get into his van. I looked. He had not locked the doors. I continued talking to him and called for backup as I was working the handle of the door. I told the man this was his last chance to come out. He refused. "Then I am putting you under arrest."

He hit the door lock, but I had it unlatched. The door opened. He slid across the seat, but I grabbed him by his boot and he came out. My dog came out and nailed him on the leg as he was resisting. The man yelled, "There is a dog on my leg!"

"Yeah, there is. And if you will put your hands behind your back and stop fighting, I will call him off." Brutus found a large quantity of cocaine in the van. He then went over, peed on the van's tires, and then slowly walked away from me and jumped into the cruiser.

Ask any handler, problems with our dogs just pop up. Brutus dislikes inmates and prisoners. He challenges them. We have many people who approach him every day.

He is friendly and wants to be petted unless you are an inmate or prisoner. People can be dressed any way, any gender and any personality. Brutus just knows. He has penned trustees in the corner of my office when they were cleaning. He never bites, just deeply growls. He has herded four trustees against the building when I took him outside for his break. Brutus's actions are sneakily done when I take my eyes off him for a minute. But the major one was in Chardon Municipal Court. The judge asked me to bring Brutus into court. I did and put him into a down position in the corner of the courtroom at the judge's request. We were arraigning twelve weekend prisoners. Brutus did fine for the first eleven. I watched him very diligently, but since he seemed to be listening, I started to ease off. The twelfth prisoner was called up to the bench. He was arrested for sex crimes against children. We were cautioned that he was infected with AIDS and hepatitis C. He started to walk up to the bench. My back was to Brutus; I was talking to the bailiff. I heard an excited yell. I turned to see Brutus with his nose in the guy's rear pushing him to the bench in front of the judge. I thought I was in real trouble with the growling from my dog and the screaming from the prisoner while the court was in session. The prisoner was pinned between the judge's bench and Brutus's nose. I called him to me. The judge started laughing. He told the prisoner, "Hey, do not run from Judge Brutus."

The judge asked for a picture of Brutus. It is hanging in his chambers.

Constable Bradley Gillespie

Winnipeg Police Service, Winnipeg, Canada

K-9 Utah

Brad had just driven from Winnipeg to Florida for a training week. Two other handlers had planned to share the driving but could not get time off from their superiors. I saw his Canadian cruiser drive up to the training site in a park. The handlers and dogs were practicing the muzzle walk. He was tired but very eager to begin. I ran up to him and quickly asked if he would tell me Utah's story at break time. He hesitated, gave me a huge grin, and said YES!

I have been a police officer for ten years, four years as a handler. K-9 Utah is a Malinois, a general-purpose patrol dog, cross-trained in explosives detection and emergency response team deployment. He has been successful in tracking over a hundred suspects in his career so far. I joined the police to hunt down bad guys, and that is what I get to do.

Two summers ago, I was working the evening shift with my service dog, Utah. A stolen auto pursuit commenced in the city. The drivers were wanted on several different offenses. The pursuit went through the city. By policy, I was at the rear of the other police cars in pursuit. The suspects smashed the car and bailed out and began running. We hooked up containment around the area. Utah tracked to the first suspect, the other two fled, running down toward the riverbank. We tracked them for a couple of miles; they kept running up from the river into the residential area; they would see our containment cars and run back through the houses to the river. I tracked them to a fairly major intersection. Then Utah gave me a head snap toward the river. He jumped into the river and began to swim. I put my flashlight in my mouth and began to swim behind my dog. With my flashlight, I caught sight of two sets of eyes and two noses pressed up under the underpass under the water. I was able to get Utah back before he made contact with their faces. This was my dog's best technical track as it covered so many varieties of terrain.

Officer John Lien

Moorhead Police Department, Moorhead, Minnesota
K-9 Hickok

I do not always meet the K-9 handlers in person. We become acquainted through phone calls and numerous e-mails. Often a friend of a friend will tell me there is a handler I must meet. I used to think perhaps I was just meeting the cream of the crop, but after observing training days, seminars, and riding on patrol for more than ten years, I find that a K-9 handler is a very dedicated, well-trained officer, eager to tell about his dog and their adventures together.

I've been in law enforcement since the spring of 1993. I joined the Moorhead Police Department in the fall of 1999. The city of Moorhead, bordering Fargo, North Dakota, has an estimated 33,000 people. I've been a canine handler with my department since the spring of 2004. My canine partner's name is Hickok. Ever since I was young, I was fascinated with the legendary peace officer Wild Bill Hickok, I used to spend hours reading books about him, taking the trip back in time, to his exciting and adventurous days. Shortly after I met my wife, I learned she was a distant cousin to Wild Bill. For that reason alone, I knew I had to marry her—just kidding. Years later, after being chosen to be the department's next canine handler, I had to decide on a name for my new partner. I chose the name *Hickok.*

Hickok is a four-year-old male German shepherd. He is all black in color. He isn't very large, but he makes up for his size with his quickness. He is from the Czech Republic. He and I trained together in basic canine school with the Saint Paul Police Department Canine Unit. He is certified through the U.S. Police Canine Association in general patrol, tracking, and narcotics detection.

I've learned that in order to have street success as a canine team, it is important to actively seek opportunities for canine use during street patrol. This means being active on patrol as a canine handler, or showing up at calls, without request, in case the canine may be used. Hickok and I have had some memorable moments in our canine career.

On a September 2005 evening, deputies from the Clay County Sheriff's Department requested Hickok's and my assistance with the locating of a suicidal man.

The man took an unknown number of pills and was becoming drowsy. He ran from his home into a grassy and wooded area. This area was a very small town within the county. I took my dog to the location where the man was last seen. I briefly talked with deputies who were on the scene. One of the deputies showed me where the man last ran and the time frame when he was last seen. I also learned the man was wearing maroon clothing. The deputies didn't know if he was armed with any weapons.

The terrain of the area was heavy grass, some woods, and a ditch along a paved road. Weather conditions were cool, with a mist of rain, and darkness was almost upon us.

I put Hickok into his tracking harness and accompanied the deputy to the area where the man was last seen. I knew that finding the man as soon as possible was going to be important for his well-being, due to his apparent overdose.

I had a deputy assisting me on the track. It is common procedure for canine handlers to have an officer assisting on canine tracks. That officer is responsible for watching all around the canine team during the track, in case a suspect attempts to "ambush," or somehow harm the canine team.

The handler keenly watches the canine, looking for behavior changes, which tells the handler if the canine is closing in on the suspect or person being tracked. The assisting officer also helps the canine team when and if there is an apprehension of the suspect. That officer would then take the suspect into custody, while the handler continues to control the K-9.

I gave Hickok the command TRACK, and he began to smell the ground where the man was last seen. Hickok tracked into the heavy grass area. He then lifted his head for a brief moment and began air-scenting. Because of his air-scenting, I suspected he possibly smelled someone upwind from us. Hickok continued with the track, pulling me hard and fast through the heavy grass and ravine. It was difficult to see and follow Hickok, because of the darkness and rough terrain. I kept pace with him, which for me was more like a very fast walk or slow jog. I knew we were on the man's track.

After tracking with great intensity for three hundred yards, Hickok immediately stopped on the track. Because it was dark, I had to focus on where he had stopped. To my surprise, I then saw a maroon outline of a person lying on the ground, and I saw that Hickok was standing at the feet of what turned out to be the man we were looking for.

I immediately pulled Hickok away from the man. Our intent was to locate him, not physically apprehend or have my dog "bite" him. The man was lying on his back motionless, not responding to us. Even though the man was motionless, we still didn't know if he was armed, or if he had intent to harm us. It was also difficult to see him in the darkness. I gave Hickok the command WATCH HIM, so Hickok began to bark at the man. When the deputy helping me on the track determined the man wasn't armed or a threat, I had Hickok stop barking at the man. I took him back to our patrol car. I rewarded Hickok with tons of praise, saying GOOD TRACK, and GOOD BOY. We also played tug-a-war with his favorite Kong toy.

After looking back on the incident, we found the man lying on the ground directly upwind from where Hickok initially began to air-scent at the beginning of the track. He was able to locate the man, without injuring him, possibly even helping to save his life.

I have learned that the success of a canine team is possible with the teamwork of other patrol officers. This is true not only for a successful deployment, but also for a safe deployment. I've come to realize the importance of continuous and quality canine training. When successful results come from canine deployments, it makes all the hours of training worth every minute.

Not only is Hickok an important partner to me in police work, but he is also an important part of my family. He is just like a child who doesn't want to be left behind. He comes with us on most vacations, when it is feasible for him to come along, and he behaves himself very well. He has enjoyed campfires and canoe rides as much as anyone else in my family. In fact, he has been responsible for one family canoe tip-over, by trying to catch the waves with his mouth, as we were rowing through the lake. I guess he always has had an intense play drive. We decided that the canoe probably wasn't the best place for Hickok anymore.

Being a canine handler has been the most rewarding experience in my law enforcement career. It is reassuring to know that I have a loyal partner with me while on patrol. The police canine is definitely an excellent locating tool. I know that while working on patrol, Hickok has my back at all times, and in return, I do my best to take care of him.

Customs and Airports

Border Patrol Agent Clayton Thomas

U.S. Border Patrol National Canine Facility, El Paso, Texas
K-9 JACKO

My copy of Police *magazine seemed to open to the photo of K-9 Jacko. He had just been voted the "Nation's Best Working Dog." Even with his toy in his mouth, he seemed to be smiling. As I read the article, I knew I wanted to meet his handler via e-mail. Clay was eager to talk about working with his Belgian Malinois, which had been credited with saving the lives of many illegal immigrants being smuggled across the border into the United States.*

In October 1998, I was selected to attend the U.S. Border Patrol National Canine Facility in El Paso, Texas, to become a certified canine handler. After arriving to the National Canine Facility, I remember that we had three full days of classroom lectures before we even got to see our dogs, much less know which one would be assigned to us. The anxiety and anticipation were almost too much. Finally, we were taken to the kennels and given our canine assignments. I was assigned a forty-two-pound male Belgian Malinois named Jacko. The U.S. Border Patrol dogs are trained to locate the odor of marijuana, cocaine, heroin, methamphetamine, and concealed humans. I remember walking up to the gate of Jacko's kennel and seeing this little skinny dog poised at the door as if to say, "Hey, get me out of here." I reached my fingers through the fence, and he came over for a few token scratches behind the ears.

Shortly thereafter, we were told to head back to the classroom for more lectures. As I stood up at the kennel door to leave, Jacko came unglued. He began to spin in circles, bark, and jump so high that you thought he might leap right out of the kennel.

Jacko and I successfully completed our six weeks of training, became certified, and entered on duty to Alpine, Texas, in November 1998. After a while of living good and working Alpine, we got Jacko up to his true weight of about fifty to fifty-five pounds.

In Alpine, our work consisted mainly of conducting traffic observation duties on two different highways, and traffic-check duties at two low-volume checkpoints. We also responded to other agency call-outs and did search warrants for the narcotics task force. K-9 Jacko and I spent nearly three years in Alpine together and had many successes. In July 2001, I was promoted to senior patrol agent and transferred to Sierra Blanca, Texas.

K-9 Jacko and I entered on duty at Sierra Blanca on July 1, 2001. This was an extremely exciting move for me as Sierra Blanca operates a high-volume checkpoint on I-10 coming out of El Paso. I had been detailed to Sierra Blanca several times while I was stationed in Alpine for operational enhancement details. So, I knew what I was getting into. I remember the first night that Jacko and I worked in Sierra Blanca.

We were assigned to the swing shift on a busy Tuesday night. As the thousands of semis, passenger cars, buses, recreational vehicles, and whatever else decided to drive up came through, I remember looking at Jacko and seeing that he was a little overwhelmed with it all. We worked very hard together, with a lot of help from the great agents in Sierra Blanca, to get him trained up and accustomed to working the high volume and intensity of the workload. It wasn't long before Jacko figured out the so-called "game" of working the checkpoint as a dog, and from there we never looked back. K-9 Jacko and I apprehended over six hundred cases during our career together. The following are some of the more memorable experiences, accomplishments, and seizures that I had with Jacko.

His first load—no matter what the load is, a handler will always remember the first load. We had been in the field together nearly a month and hadn't caught anything. I was getting frustrated watching the other handlers from my K-9 class catch their first loads. I remember that I was on the day shift working traffic observations on Highway 118 south of Alpine with one of the senior agents in the station.

We had been working the traffic pretty hard all morning and were still coming up with a goose egg. Shortly after noon, we observed an SUV pass us traveling north. After making sure that we had the suspicion necessary, we stopped the truck just north of Study Butte, Texas. While conducting the nonintrusive exterior sniff of the vehicle, I noticed Jacko alert. The excitement was incredible, seeing it for the first time out of a training environment. A search of the vehicle revealed over 170 pounds of marijuana hidden in the rear walls of the truck.

At the border crossing, the agent takes a point; this refers to where he checks traffic and immigration status. We run the K-9s as the traffic is pulling into this checkpoint. When an agent feels that there is a need to investigate someone's immigration status further or a K-9 alerts to a vehicle, the point agent sends the vehicle from the primary point area to the secondary inspection area for further investigation.

Another load that comes to mind happened while I was working the checkpoint on I-10 near Sierra Blanca. I remember that I was working a swing shift, which was always the busiest shift. Traffic had been a nightmare all night long. While working the primary position with Jacko, I noticed a little break in the never-ending line of traffic.

I started checking the vehicles as quickly as I could. A flatbed semi pulled up with what appeared to be a load of lumber. The load was covered with a tarp and had lots of tie-down straps and bungee cords. During the immigration inspection, Jacko dragged me down the side of the flatbed and alerted underneath the large tarp-covered cargo. I remember thinking, *Man, there's going to be a lot of dope in there!*

After getting the vehicle into the secondary area, the other agents and I began inspecting the load. The load was pretty heavily fortified with the tie-downs, and we were having a hard time getting them all off. After spending a considerable amount of time loosening the straps, I finally had the rear end of the cargo open. I noticed that the load wasn't a load of lumber but was instead a large crate.

Now I was really excited because lumber would have been hollowed out in the middle somewhere, you only have to fill up a crate. The bigger the vehicle, the bigger the load, right? So, I pried the side of the crate open and discovered one of the most horrific things I had seen up to this point in my career. I was expecting to see bundles of narcotics and instead was surprised by several sets of eyeballs and the overwhelming stench of people crammed inside of the crate. We rushed to open the rear of the crate and helped all of the illegal aliens out. After checking the aliens, we found that they were all OK. Hot, tired, and thirsty, but nonetheless OK. Twenty-eight people in all were saved from what surely may have been another tragedy like the one that occurred in Victoria, Texas.

Approximately an hour later, one of the agents working the primary referred a semi into the secondary location for a K-9 sniff. As I walked into secondary, I noticed that the semi and flatbed trailer were nearly the same as the one I had apprehended earlier. Once again, Jacko alerted to the flatbed with the large tarped crate on the back. We opened the crate and located twenty-one more illegal aliens trapped inside with no possible way of escaping. This is probably the most rewarding load that I remember getting with Jacko. In one night, Jacko potentially saved the lives of forty-nine people.

During this same time of year, we had been extremely busy and had been catching a lot of humans and narcotics. For this load, it was almost the same setting, working a swing shift. Traffic was so heavy that we were having to wave most of it through the checkpoint for safety. It was just after 9:30 p.m., and we were all really tired from working several very long shifts in the prior days. Once again, while working primary with Jacko, we got a little break in the traffic. I quickly started checking as many vehicles as possible before we got overwhelmed with traffic again. As I was checking a passenger vehicle, I noticed Jacko alert further down the on ramp. I cleared the vehicle on point and began inspecting the next vehicle. Jacko cleared the vehicle on point and continued alerting down the ramp. The next vehicle was a semi with a regular box trailer. As I was talking to the driver, Jacko dragged me down to the front of the semitrailer and alerted to the front drain hole. Once we had the semi in secondary, we discovered several boxes hidden among the pallets of tile. The first few boxes we opened were found to have bundles of marijuana. I did a quick count of the boxes and estimated that we had about two thousand pounds or so. Catching the ton-plus loads happened on a pretty regular basis, so we got pretty good at our guesses. As we were unloading the boxes, one of the agents had the bottom of a box break. As he picked up the bundles, he noticed that it wasn't marijuana. It happened to be cocaine. So, we unloaded all of the boxes and went through them all very carefully. In the end, this load ended up being 1,320 pounds of marijuana and 721 pounds of cocaine. The estimated wholesale value of this load was over $24,000,000. Not bad for one night's work with Jacko!

I remember coming in on a midnight shift in Alpine, Texas. As I walked in the door the phone was ringing. The Fort Stockton Border

Patrol station was requesting a canine to sniff a car at the Pecos County Sheriff's Office. The car had been traveling west on I-10. About an hour or so later, I arrived in Fort Stockton.

I noticed K-9 Jacko alert to the dashboard. After taking the dashboard apart, I found several bundles wrapped in gray duct tape. The end result was $120,000 in contaminated cash. If there is a large sum of money being transported, you would normally have proof of payment, deposit, winnings, etc. to prove it is yours. Or you would secure it by making it into a check or money order, or have it transferred into different accounts. Also if you are transporting $100,000, you would not wrap it in duct tape, disassemble the interior of your car, and conceal it inside.

There is a procedure to prove that money is contaminated solely based on the K-9 alert which will stand up in court. After this is completed, the appropriate agency is contacted to collect the money. The person caught with the money just needs to provide proof that the money is theirs and legally obtained. Any honest person will be able to do this. More often than not, it is drug money and the person has no proof of deposit, earnings, winnings, etc. They are issued a receipt for the money. I think the federal law states that you can carry up to $10,000 without having to prove anything. So, the end result was that we seized the cash, gave the guy a receipt, but turned him loose, and then it was up to him to go back to the drug people and explain how we took his money and he did not get arrested. Probably not too good for the person transporting the cash.

One of the most memorable loads was also K-9 Jacko's largest marijuana load. We were working a midnight shift and traffic was pretty slow. I went out to take a point near the end of the shift. In the middle of my point, a semi came through for inspection. As I talked to the driver, I noticed K-9 Jacko alert to the front drain hole of the trailer.

The driver said that the load was going to the East Coast and that it was some kind of military or industrial steel containers. Inside the trailer, we found four large steel containers that were palletized and wrapped in plastic. Everything looked legitimate except for Jacko's alert. I had to make the call to either open all of the containers, which would ruin the valuable load, or let it go. The first rule of being a K-9 handler is to trust your dog. So I did just that.

I called the head of my station and told him what I had. K-9 Jacko and I had caught so many loads that we had gained the confidence of my superiors. My boss asked me if I felt confident that there would be something there.

I told him that I was confident in Jacko's alert but I had just wanted to run it by him before we started dismantling the valuable cargo. Without hesitation, my boss said, "If you are confident, I trust you and let's do it." He arrived at the checkpoint a short while later to help with the dismantling. Each of the containers had numerous large bolts sealing the two sections shut that our air impact wrenches were struggling to loosen.

We finally got all of the bolts off one of the containers and found that we were unable to separate the two parts with a large pry bar. We decided to use the Jaws of Life to try and separate them. The Jaws of Life struggled to separate the parts more than an inch. But it opened just enough for me to get a knife inside and stab a bundle of what was later found to be marijuana. We used a forklift to unload all four containers and finally hours later got them all taken apart. The result was 4,475 pounds of marijuana. A great lesson of why we trust our dogs.

Since I mentioned Jacko's first load, I also feel it necessary to mention one of his last large loads. I was working a day shift and was working primary with another agent. As we talked and checked the morning traffic, I noticed K-9 Jacko alert to a small moving truck. I advised the agent on point that I had an alert.

She told me that the driver was nervous and was giving her some story about moving back to college. The guy looked like a college kid, and the items in the truck matched the story, furniture, appliances, plants, clothes, etc.

Trust your dog! We started unloading the items in the back and discovered a wall of marijuana buried about halfway into the truck. The result was over 3,200 pounds of marijuana. Not bad for an old dog.

In March 2005, I was on operational detail at the San Ysidro Port of Entry in San Ysidro, California. I was contacted by my superiors at the National Canine Facility and advised that they needed me to update statistics on K-9 Jacko, as I was nominated to represent the Border Patrol for the "Paws to Recognize" National Canine of the Year Award. We ended up being selected to represent the Border Patrol and the CBP (U.S. Customs and Border Protection).

We were up against four other highly qualified canines from around the country. We traveled to New York City for the award ceremony. K-9 Jacko had received nearly half of the online votes and was named Canine of the Year for 2005. His paw prints are enshrined at the Canine Hall of Fame in Los Angeles, California.

The ultimate reward—first of all to represent my peers and then to have my canine selected as the number one dog in the country. As I told many people, I felt fortunate to have been selected to represent my peers, the U.S. Customs and Border Patrol agents, but that any of the canines on the U.S. Border Patrol could have won the same award. We were merely the representatives.

We also represented the U.S. Border Patrol on the USS *Intrepid* in New York City on the National Recognition Day for Working Canines hosted by Dr. Jane Goodall. Then we got to travel to Washington, D.C., to conduct a canine demonstration in open session in front of Congress. What an honor and thrill that was! Jacko loved the limelight and being in the front of cameras.

I retired K-9 Jacko when I was selected as supervisory Border Patrol agent. I always wanted to be able to retire him and let him lie in the sun and play with all the toys he can handle and just be a dog for once in his life.

I was worried about him, though. All he had ever known was going to work with me and searching cars all day. I wondered how he would handle the change of seeing me get ready for work and leave without him. I feel that he handled it as well as could be expected. He did a lot of sleeping and looking for the sun coming through the windows. But when I got home, it was time for play. Then in July 2006, I was lucky enough to be selected as permanent staff canine instructor at the National Canine Facility in El Paso.

Jacko was now allowed to come to work with me and be utilized as a canine for instructional purposes for new handlers and instructors. We also do the demonstrations for all of the high-profile visits from the commissioner of CBP, various senators, congressmen and Border Patrol Chief, etc.

Even though K-9 Jacko is getting old and is getting gray, he is still as good as ever when it comes to work. In his old age, he has relaxed and become even more of a lovable guy who has truly found the meaning of enjoying life. Being a canine handler and instructor with K-9 Jacko has been the most rewarding and memorable experience of my working career. Thank you for the opportunity to share some of the memories with Jacko.

Officer Eddie Martinez

Los Angeles Airport Police, Los Angeles, California
K-9s RALF AND MARCO

I wonder if anything could compare with the thrill of being a passenger in a police cruiser driving down the huge tarmac of LAX. I had to assume those pilots in the huge jets could see us. But it was obvious that Eddie knew his patrol area, so there was no danger. The noise of jet engines filled my ears. I could not wait to tell my family what I had been doing! Inside LAX, the crowds of people stepped aside giving Eddie and Ralf room to patrol the terminal as I tagged along with them. I saw many things that for public safety I could not use in my book.

At LAX (Los Angeles International Airport), there are two police departments, LAXPD and LAPD. Ralf and I work for the Los Angeles Airport Police. We belong to LAXPD/LAPD K-9 Task Force. We have the same mission to keep the airport and passengers safe. I had two dogs before Ralf, but they did not work out, because their play drive was not strong enough to work for their rewards. In essence, those two dogs were not good enough to be bomb detection dogs.

The first year I was with Ralf, we were at an air show with crowds of people asking if they could pet him. I finally put him in a SIT position. A little girl about head level with Ralf asked if she could pet him. Her mother had told her that Ralf was a police dog. For some reason, Ralf likes to lick little kids' faces. When the little girl began petting Ralf; he licked her face. The mother told her, "He is kissing you." The crowd just melted!

I do have a lot of interaction with kids. When I walk through the airport terminal, I have to be really careful because kids don't know any better, they like to pull on my dog or pet him without my permission. Ralf is a very big dog, so he could accidentally hurt someone or even get injured himself. People must understand they cannot pet my dog without permission from me, especially when he is working. That is why I always warn people never to crowd a dog they are not familiar with. Ralf likes attention when he is not working. He will put his paw out for you to hold. When you let go, he will put it up again. People think I taught him to shake hands, but he naturally does that on his own. When my friend K-9 Officer Alfonso Lagos approaches, Ralf will put out his paw, and Alfonso will hold it and greet Ralf.

Sometimes when I get the police car washed, I will leave Ralf at home and forget that he is not in the back. This is embarrassing to say but it is a habit of mine to talk to Ralf when he is inside the cruiser with me, so sometimes I find myself talking to myself.

It is truly an art form to see a handler work and train with his dog. The trainer can motivate his dog to do things for him because of the bond they have formed together. By watching Ralf's body language, I know what he is doing or how he is feeling. I know when he is sick or when he is happy. After two years of working with Ralf, we began really working as a team. I was taught that if a handler is nervous it goes down the leash to the dog, so in general, dogs are very good at "reading" body language and sensing when something is wrong with Dad. Ralf and I are very good at reading each other's body language without saying a word. So when I search, I try to keep everything consistent and simple, so as not to confuse Ralf.

I was called to a restaurant inside the terminal for unattended luggage. We cleared the area, and I had Ralf sniff the luggage. I made sure to clear a small area of the restaurant, so Ralf could work without distractions. While Ralf was sniffing the luggage, I was a little concerned, as he was showing a lot of interest in the luggage as he kept sniffing. I made sure my body language did not give him a clue to alert. If I stopped moving, Ralf might think, *Dad has stopped, so that means something is here, so I will sit, so I can get my reward.* After three or four seconds of sniffing, Ralf walked away. Based on my training and experience, I was confident the luggage was safe.

When the owner returned to claim the suitcase, she was told that she must pay more attention. By leaving her bag unattended, she could have caused the terminal to be shut down. In my opinion, the reason Ralf was showing a lot of interest on the suitcase was because he smelled an animal odor or odor that was very interesting to him. The owner told me that her dog had slept on the luggage the night before her trip. Ralf was just being a dog! That was the interesting odor for Ralf—another dog's odor. Odor that is new or interesting to a dog is what we handlers call "novel odor." When he smells explosive odors, Ralf's behavior changes. I am the only one who can recognize that change. That is the reason training and bonding with your dog is so very important. Only the handler can interpret his dog's body language and behavior. I noticed everyone was watching Ralf; it was like a show for them. Ralf got applause from the onlookers, and then we were off to the next radio call.

We did bite training at a museum. Inside there was a man-made waterfall. Another officer dressed in a bite suit as the "bad guy" was on the other side of the waterfall encouraging Ralf to attack. To get to the "suspect," Ralf would have to go through the waterfall and cross through the two-foot deep water. I knew Ralf would have to get wet. I gave the command to Ralf; he took a couple of steps, then stopped to look at me. The command was not working, so I went into the water. Suddenly, the picture was clear to him. He seemed to say, "OK, Dad!" He went into the water, but he kept looking back over his shoulder to see if I was still with him. I got soaking wet head to toe. Finally, after running through the water, he got a good bite and held on strongly to the "suspect" in the bite suit. I was so proud of him. GOOD BOY! He did what he was supposed to do. That particular exercise was designed to build confidence in the K-9 and the handler's trust in his dog. I always trusted Ralf.

Our K-9 unit was told that advanced training was being offered by the Transportation Security Administration (TSA) at Lackland Air Force Base in San Antonio, Texas. Our sergeant asked us who wanted to go. We would have to give our current dogs to another handler. Once we were at the base, a new dog would be assigned to us. Handlers from many states across the United States attended this training. My friend Alfonso and I were chosen as well as an LAPD officer. Both my wife and I were sad to lose Ralf to another handler, but he would be happy continuing his same work at LAX. Ralf was a good partner. I will never forget him.

We began our training at Lackland Air Force Base. My new dog is Marco. We worked and trained together for three months. Marco is a highly trained bomb detection dog. He is a single-purpose dog trained to sniff for explosives. He is not trained to sniff for drugs, lost people, or apprehend suspects. We have worked together for two years that have been challenging but very fulfilling. Every year, we must pass a series of tests in order to be certified by TSA. If a K-9 team passes the certification, the team continues to work at LAX; if not, the team cannot work in the airport environment until training issues have been addressed. The certification is a series of problems given over the course of a week. The K-9 team of handler and dog must pass with an excellent and outstanding performance.

Sergeant Blair E. Lindsay

Supervisor, K-9 Unit, Los Angeles Airport Police
Los Angeles, California

Blair was the first sergeant I had met whose main job was to supervise the large K-9 unit. His office is often a noisy, happy place where the handlers check in between assignments. Huge bags of dog food are in one corner. It is just so great to be with people who love what they do. I admit I am still in awe when I am invited "behind the scenes" in a bustling place like LAX.

My main function as a supervisor for the K-9 unit is, of course, the usual: keep track of records, supervise the K-9 handlers, and so on. But what is unusual is that now I supervise the K-9s, too. I keep track of their medical, training, and usage records. It had been said that a sergeant is jack-of-all-trades. I feel I am that plus the kitchen sink.

What I wanted to know the most as a K-9 unit supervisor was what a K-9 team could do and what their limitations were. Luckily, I was able to attend the same classes that the handlers went through. I got an understanding of how the team works together and what the handlers must go through to get the job done. But the most important was what the K-9 unit was able to do for my department.

One of the most important functions I have is in the training aspect of my job. I make sure each team is kept current in their training requirements by planning and running the scenarios. Each scenario tests a different aspect of a team's ability to perform their duties. Scenarios are fun but serious. Training is designed to simulate what could happen out on the street. A handler and K-9 can be easily hurt if safety is not considered. These teams are extremely valuable, and any injury to either partner can put a team out of service for long periods of time. There is a saying that it is not a matter whether you get bit, but when! I remember one time during training a handler was agitating another handler's K-9. As he turned away, the dog reached out and touched him. I watched as the dog sliced open a four-inch cut along the handler's upper forearm, all the while the handler not realizing that he had been bitten.

Handlers hurt in the line of duty are of great concern. Patrol K-9s are trained to protect their handlers. Unfortunately, there is not a way to duplicate in training what would happen if a handler were seriously injured. A K-9 would protect his partner, not realizing we were there to help. Several methods can be used to handle this problem. I try to foster a relationship with each and every K-9, so they will trust me and hopefully follow a command I would give them. Their basic instinct is to protect their injured partner from anyone.

Why do I put myself through all this extra work? Is it the fun? Well, yes, it is fun. Is it to work with man's best friend? Well, yes, that, too. But the number one reason is because like every police officer out there it is for the public that we serve. These animals save lives, time, and valuable public resources.

Lieutenant Guy Painter

Los Angeles Airport Police, Los Angeles, California

I met Guy at his office, a crowded Quonset hut, shared with his captain and another officer. Guy set up the meeting with the airport K-9 handlers for me. He gave me the royal treatment, a personal tour of the airport. He has become one of our favorite friends. The Los Angeles World Airports consist of Los Angeles International, Ontario International, Palmdale Regional, and Van Nuys General Aviation Airports. All four are owned by the city of Los Angeles. Guy has transferred to Ontario International where he is the assistant commanding officer of police services. His duties consist of overseeing the daily operations and especially the K-9 bomb detection unit. He attends K-9 conferences across the country, including the annual National Explosives Detection K-9 team programs.

My high school counselor said I would never amount to anything. I ran into him a few years ago and asked if he knew me. He replied that I was probably a former student. I told him, I am a police lieutenant. He seemed pretty impressed. I told him I handled *Air Force One* security as well as all the foreign heads of state who flew into our airports. I could tell he did not believe me.

Half of my career has been in traffic and half in dignitary protection. I have had fun. I was assigned to the State Department for a year and also to the Secret Service. All of the various task forces I could not have done anywhere else. I had a blast doing it, too!

In the early years, we worked on some of the rooftops. We would watch burglary suspects, the narcotic suspects, and auto thieves. Since we are located by the ocean, the rooftops can get very cold. Even in the summertime, the fog would roll in, covering us with a damp cold. We dressed in snowmobile suits in Southern California in the summertime.

I like to work here as I have always had a great staff to work with, and great bosses. LAX (Los Angeles International Airport) is one of the busiest airports in the world. Nearly 2,500 airplanes take off and land here every day. More than 60,000 passengers pass through LAX each year. A lot of foreign travelers come in and out and are over-trusting.

For example, in Japan there is not that much crime as we know it. You could leave a bag, come back the next day, and it would still be there. You could leave a wallet, and it would still be there. Here, they are as trusting as they are at home. The types of crimes at LAX are no different from anywhere else in a major city.

When 9/11 occurred, the FAA mandated that all aircraft must land regardless of where they were. We have what is called security requirements. There are five different levels. We moved up to level four, which meant we could not allow vehicles to stay at the curb and could not leave vehicles unattended. Any one that was unattended had to be searched and impounded immediately.

We could not allow vehicles of certain shapes or sizes to be in the parking structure walls that faced the terminals. A possible blast might occur from a bomb of some sort. The only thing we could do was to shut down the entire airport. From 9/11 to the week before Thanksgiving, we were shut down. I have a photo of us walking down the middle of the terminal area because it was all empty. This is my twentieth year, and that was the first time I had seen it shut down like that. It was very quiet.

We opened up a bit to allow commercial vehicles in next to the curb to bring people in and out when the flights resumed. But the further outer lanes were kept for vehicles to get into the parking structures. They had to be searched and checked with mirrors and a bomb dog. That was the only way to let vehicles back into the terminal areas.

We did allow commercial vehicles at curbside. People did not understand because taxi drivers are usually foreigners, Middle Easterners. But what the public did not realize was that all the taxi drivers had background checks on file. The cab drivers understood, and they were cooperative. When the traveling public sees them, they do not know of the requirements for the drivers. Often the cab drivers get a hard time, just like everywhere else.

LAX is the third busiest airport in the world and third in the United States in passenger count. We are number one in cargo in the entire world. Terrorists can use an airplane as a missile, but no one seems to think about cargo as a terrorist weapon.

Most of the security around the airport deals with passengers. Very little deals with cargo—very little.

What is under your seat in an airplane? People do not realize that the entire underside of their aircraft is all cargo. Not just your suitcases, but cargo. We make money shipping cargo. Now, if I cannot get somewhere in a car I just don't go—except for the couple of times I had to fly to D.C.

Where were the last couple of aircraft explosions? Most of the disasters in aircraft have been in cargo. The Florida Everglades explosion was from oxygen tanks stored in the cargo. They were not supposed to be shipped that way; it was a combination of overlooked and allowed. Pan Am Flight 108 over Lockerbie, Scotland, was from cargo.

The airport police should be able to cover this, but I do not have the manpower. I wish I did. Where does the public want me to put my officers? We cannot raise the ticket prices all the time to pay for more manpower.

The reality of business is that it is in business for profit. If they spend less on security, they can spend more on aircrafts to fly more people to make more money. They would rather do that than pay for security.

How much of your freedom are you willing to give up to help stop terrorism? Are we going to body X-ray everyone? Are you willing to stand in lines to have your bags checked? Are you willing to put up with such things as body cavity searches? The point is how much are you willing to give up, so you can visit your mother more safely? Are you willing to by-pass all of that and drive three or four days because you are afraid to fly?

Body scans and such are great technology, but I do not want people to feel they live in a Nazi state. I do not want to know everyone's background. I do not want to know what is inside their suitcases, but we have gotten to the point of intruding on everyone's rights. We need to do some reasonable searches.

When you put your suitcase on the belt, you have just consented to have it searched. If you try to take it off, they will stop you. You will say you did not know it could be "probable cause." How many civil rights are we stepping on just because someone in the Middle East might do something that may or may not have an effect on us?

We will never be the same after 9/11. It will happen again; I can guarantee you that. There have been incidents since then that have been averted; some could have had disastrous consequences in the California area, but they were stopped! Yes, the terrorists are still alive and well and still planning attacks. There have been a few who were arrested recently, and their cases are still pending. Materials to make explosives are still being found. Intelligence has been found when the arrests were made. They had maps, photos, schedules and much, much more. The bad guys overseas are also still very active.

Some of the pilots wish to be armed. I do not like that. I want the pilot to be in total control of the aircraft. The pilots often do not have the time on firing range to qualify as a police officer must. To qualify, they would have to spend time without pay on their own time to be able to carry a firearm to work.

My department supplies all the officers needed for the protection when *Air Force One* or *Air Force Two* or any head of state flies into LAX. I did that for eight years. I was the boss for three of those years. There isn't a living president who doesn't know my name. That is a bit scary to me. A former president, even when he is out of office, still has time to remember my name. I think is quite a tribute that I simply cannot fathom.

When I was still a sergeant, I was asked to do a public broadcasting service for CBS. I had to wear a microphone for an entire weekend. It took three entire days. It ran as a three-hour special on how LAX works.

The weekend they chose to film was one I had been working on for weeks. President Clinton would be arriving aboard *Air Force One*. A military transport arrived in advance, the presidential limos aboard. At nearby Van Nuys Airport, the president of Armenia was arriving. We have a separate police unit dedicated to protecting the heads of state.

If anything should go wrong, I would be the one to testify in front of Congress. That is something I never want to do, so that is why I worried so much. Yes, I do have an ulcer. The Armenian president's plane was an hour and forty minutes late. I had to cut it very close to get back to LAX for President Clinton's arrival. Everything was in place. We did a sweep of the runway and shut down all the service roads. The runways would be shut down when *Air Force One* arrived. My team kept a lookout for anything out of the ordinary. There was a high level of security. I was promoted to lieutenant soon after that!

Now as the assistant commanding officer at the LA/Ontario International Airport, I oversee the daily operations of the airport police. One of my main responsibilities is to oversee the K-9 explosives detection unit at this airport. The unit consists of six K-9 officers, their dogs, and a sergeant. These officers are one of the top K-9 units in the nation. I am responsible for ensuring they meet their training requirements, utilization goals, and their budget.

This team is constantly being called upon by other outside agencies, such as the California Highway Patrol, Ontario Police Department, Fontana Police Department, and many others. While attending K-9 conferences, it is always nice to hear our agency's name being mentioned as a model for such units.

One of my major concerns is the health and welfare of the dogs themselves. It seems as though I am constantly receiving a veterinarian bill for one of the dogs, whether for a regular checkup or an emergency visit. It seems as though the bills never stop coming. I stress to their handlers that prevention is paramount.

Another major concern is keeping the K-9 cars up and running. The cars are constantly running with the air-conditioning on whenever a dog is inside. Since the temperature gets very warm very fast here, we try to keep the dogs cool. This causes quite a bit of wear and tear on the vehicles.

Purchasing new vehicles can become quite a chore. We have to purchase our cars whenever the airport orders new cars for the fleet. This process can take up to a year. It does not take into account when a K-9 car goes down or is not repairable. Since the cars are outfitted specially for the dogs and their equipment, it seems like a battle every time we need to replace a K-9 car.

Recently, I had the unpleasantness of pulling K-9 Bento out of service. He had been our top dog, but he had bitten several people, including his handler. I could not risk him biting a citizen. Bad enough that I have a scar from him. People always want to pet our dogs, and it really bothers a handler when he has to tell someone that his dog can't be petted. K-9 Dok is the replacement dog, and he loves being petted and will lick every one to death, given the chance to do so. His handler is much happier now that people can pet his dog.

K-9 Bento is now working with the military and has been in Iraq for three months. It is nice to know that when I get a call asking if our dogs are available, the calling agencies trust our dogs to perform.

World Trade Center 9/11

Major Paul B. Morgan

U.S. Army, Retired
Jupiter, Florida/Osterville, Massachusetts
K-9 Cody Bear

Major Morgan is a former Green Beret and paratrooper in the 82nd Airborne Division. He served in Vietnam in 1965 as a Ranger Advisor with the 30th ARVN Ranger Battalion. There he traded a .38 caliber pistol and a set of sterling silver rosary beads to a French priest for a German shepherd named Suzie. That dog would not only save his life but ignite a passion for working with other dogs in his own K-9 security business for twenty years. Paul has written two books, K-9 Soldiers: Vietnam *and* After the Parrot's Beak: U.S. Operations in Cambodia.*

Paul Morgan and Hal Wilson had seen combat in Vietnam, but it was nothing like the destruction that they saw at the World Trade Center when they arrived with their search-and-rescue K-9s to help on September 12, 2001.

9/11 had happened. Mayor Giuliani had warned the public, "Uniforms only! No gawkers allowed!"

I called my marine buddy, Hal Wilson. "Hal, get your BDUs and dog and meet me at the train! Let's roll!" (BDUs refers to battle dress uniform.)

"Aye, aye, Skipper," he responded.

My camouflage battle dress uniform was in my closet, so I put it on and headed to Ground Zero with my golden retriever, Cody Bear.

The next morning we were on our way into the "pile of rubble," riding the train into Penn Station with our dogs, Cody and Sue. We had to walk two miles to Ground Zero—past one roadblock after another. There must have been hundreds of people on the street, perhaps thousands. The silence was deafening, no cars, no trucks, just people pressing against police barricades, trying to get closer to the columns of black smoke at the south end of Manhattan.

In camouflage battle dress we passed each roadblock, directed by NYPD officers to West Street and Ground Zero. On the way in, a news reporter stopped Hal and me asking, "Give me three reasons why you are doing this?" Hal had that angry look and that thousand-meter stare combat veterans display after too much time on the line. I told the reporter, "Duty, honor, country," and he left us alone.

My buddy Hal Wilson and I went into the pile of rubble at the World Trade Center with our search dogs, Cody and Sue, at 11 a.m. on Wednesday, September 12, 2001. You wouldn't believe the teamwork and the silence with hundreds of firefighters stumbling through the mess.

Hal was a U.S. Marine in Vietnam while I served with the 82nd Airborne. I never thought a paratrooper and a marine would get along so well together. In our camouflage battle dress, we were the first military personnel on site because the airports, the tunnels, and many other roads to New York City were closed.

On the way in through the rubble, we walked past deserted restaurants with red-and-white-checkered tablecloths, fully stocked bars, wine on tables and menus in hallways that had survived. Then the realization hit us head-on as we entered a courtyard and we saw the "pile" of debris several stories high.

We linked up with four state police K-9 teams, which were the dirtiest, filthiest men and dogs we had ever seen. They were covered with gray dust and mud. All of the troopers had that thousand-meter stare. The troopers and their dirty dogs were being pulled out as Hal and I were deployed with Cody and Sue to the "pile," stacked several stories high with fire rigs, police cars, twisted I-beams, shards of glass, aluminum, wood, and chunks of metal and concrete sticking out of the ground. The metal rods I stumbled through reminded me of the punji sticks in Vietnam.

The fire lieutenant in charge led Hal and I and our dogs to a fire rig, which had been a hose truck. It was gray, completely burned out . . . no seats, dash, steering wheel . . . nothing.

"Get down there, please, and let me know if you can detect anybody in there!" the officer requested.

Cody and I climbed down ten feet, and I called into the truck. "If you can hear me, say One. If you can hear me, say Two, if you can hear me, say Three." There was no response. Then I repeated myself and said, "If you can hear me but can't talk, bang the wall with your foot once, twice, three times." Still no response. Cody, my golden retriever, began scratching, and I told the firefighters above me, "We have a body down here!"

They pulled Cody and me out of the pit and began cutting the truck open with an electric saw. Several minutes later, I heard the firefighters below call out, "Body bag!" As an orange plastic roll was passed down the line into the pit next to the burned-out rig, another officer asked me, "How good is your dog?"

We were standing on a hose line, and Cody was scratching again. I didn't have to answer the officer when Cody's paws suddenly were covered with blood. "Body bag!" was heard again and another roll of orange plastic was passed down the line. The remains of the first firefighter were carefully lifted to the surface in a basket. Eight of his brothers carried the remains to the morgue truck. Soon the second firefighter's remains that Cody had discovered were placed into another body bag, and we were asked to step aside as another crew removed them.

Another officer grabbed my arm and directed me to a concrete slab, which had been a wall the day before. Under the slab was another fire rig. "Can you get down there and tell us if . . ." He did not have to finish the request. A hole had been punched into the wall of the debris below the slab.

"What's down there?" somebody asked. Cody and I climbed down into this pit, and I stuck my nose into the hole, smelling gas. Then Cody passed by me, digging into the debris under the slab. We smelled burned flesh again, and I signaled the officer behind me. "Body bag!" was heard again. I couldn't believe Cody had discovered three sets of remains in thirty minutes. It was more than I had ever expected from that dog.

As I tried to get out from under the slab and clear the way for another crew to remove remains, I found myself in a great deal of trouble. I was wedged into a pit and couldn't move. It was like being under a staircase in a dark basement, and there was no way to get out. Cody was still in front of me, however, and in his dash for safety, gasping for air, he jumped over my left shoulder and turned me around. I crawled toward the light, and we were lifted to the surface by a squad of firefighters.

I was exhausted by this time, so Cody and I returned to the top of the "pile," watching a body bag with remains being removed from the scene every twenty minutes or so. Soon a wind picked up, and we began dodging shrapnel flying off the buildings around the pile. I thought I had seen it all in two years of Vietnam combat. I hadn't.

I couldn't find my helmet, which was buried in my backpack under the three days of rations I had loaded for Cody. "Helmets" was the order, so I stumbled away to the relative safety of another structure (one which collapsed later in the day) where two nurses gave us water and another provided us a cup of orange juice. Then I got rattled, starting to look for my partner, Hal, and his dog. He was right behind me with Sue. "Hey, Marine . . . let's get the hell out of here!" I shouted. "Yes, sir!" he responded, and we followed a crew of firefighters carrying remains from the pile through the building with the bar and restaurants out to the morgue truck.

We were exhausted and hurting. Cody was sneezing and coughing, so we headed for the Suffolk County SPCA van. But before we left the scene, Hal procured a metal tray from a garbage pile, and we gave our dogs all the water we had, and as we did, a squad of firefighters behind us poured all of their water into the tray for the dogs. No one said a word.

After the dogs were checked out by volunteer vets and vet techs who washed their paws and eyes, and received shots, we were ordered to rest for an hour at Stuyvesant High School. We followed orders.

About 4 p.m. we started home, walking toward Penn Station on 34th Street. Sue was close to heat exhaustion, and Cody was having a hard time breathing. We spotted a Franciscan priest who blessed the animals, Hal, and me. We felt better and started on our way again. Cody stopped in his tracks on 23rd Street and 6th Avenue, unable to walk any longer. We watered both dogs, taking a break on the sidewalk, leaning against an office building. A passerby said, "Thanks!" After a few minutes, we were on our way again.

When we arrived at Penn Station, twenty minutes before our train was due to depart for Long Island, more people said, "Thanks!" providing us with food, water, and a couple of beers. On the train ride home, Cody slept under my foot with his back to the air-conditioning. Thanks, New Yorkers, for giving us a chance to help! Honor, Duty, Country!

State Park Officer John Patrick

Ohio Department of Resources, Region IV
Caesar Creek State Park and Little Miami State Park
South of Dayton, Ohio
K-9s GUESE AND YOGI

---

*John started the K-9 program in his department with his K-9
Guese. His dog is trained in narcotic detection, tracking, area
search, article search, crowd control, cadaver location, and handler protection. That is a lot for any dog.*

It was a cool April night. I had just graduated from K-9 school a few days
earlier. It was my first K-9 call. It was about 2 a.m. A sheriff's deputy
had stopped a vehicle for a possible DWI violation. As the deputy was
attempting to arrest the driver, a scuffle ensued. While they were on the
ground, the suspect was able to grab a rock and strike the deputy in the
head with it. The suspect than ran into the night. The deputy was able to
see him jump into the Little Miami River and saw him swimming toward
the other side. "Get me a K-9" is what I heard on the radio.

When I arrived in the area, I decided to start my search on the
side of the river that the deputy last saw the suspect swimming toward.
After crossing a cornfield and arriving at the riverbank, I made three
announcements into the darkness for the suspect to "speak to me or I
will send the dog."

Hearing no response, I deployed K-9 Guese to attempt to locate the
suspect. Guese ran to the riverbank and began sniffing the air. He then
ran about three hundred yards downstream; he stopped and was staring
at the water. I had two back-up officers with me. We got to where Guese
was standing. We could see from the wet footprints in the dirt that the
suspect had gotten out of the water. At this point, I assumed he was concealed somewhere, hiding in the thick brush.

I pulled Guese away from the riverbank and tried to get him to
search the bushy area. Each time I would pull him away from the river-

bank and direct him to the bush, he would return to the riverbank and just stare at the water.

We could not figure out what he was staring at. Shining our flashlights down at the water, we could see only a tree trunk about four feet long and about one foot across, partially submerged in the river. I kept looking at it for a few minutes before I noticed the tips of some fingers on the side of the tree trunk just at the water's surface.

The suspect was hiding completely submerged with his face in an air pocket on the underside of the tree trunk. Only his fingertips were exposed. I put the leash on the dog, and we ordered the suspect to come out of the water or the dog would be sent in after him. The suspect complied and was taken into custody. He was charged with DWI, resisting arrest, and assaulting a police officer.

It dawned on me later that the reason Guese did not bark at the suspect was that we had never trained him for this type of situation where the suspect was submerged.

That was my first K-9 call. I could not have asked for a better outcome. I have no doubt we would not have located this person if the dog had not been used.

September 11, 2001. That fateful day when the terrorists attacked our country. On that day, like everyone else, I sat glued to the TV watching in vivid detail of how four commercial airplanes had been hijacked and used as weapons. I watched as the World Trade Center Twin Towers came crashing to the ground. I watched as a cloud of dust and debris enveloped the city streets of Manhattan. I watched and felt helpless.

September 14, 2001, I received a request to assist the rescuers at the World Trade Center. My K-9 Guese was cadaver-trained. Cadaver dogs were being requested to attempt to locate the bodies in the rubble. The next morning, Guese and I were on our way to the Big Apple. I had never been to New York City before. I had never worked at a large disaster site before. I had trained Guese with a few large rubble piles in the past, but I was not ready for what I saw when arriving. I must admit it was not so much as what I saw but more of what I smelled. Death. It was everywhere.

It was about 10 p.m. when I left the Convention Center with my credentials and arrived at Public School 89. My bedroom consisted of a military cot on the floor of the auditorium. Guese could either sleep on the floor beside me or in his kennel in my cruiser. I couldn't sleep. Around midnight, Guese and I walked the two blocks to the WTC site and began working.

The first set of "dog boots" that Guese wore to keep his feet from being cut by the debris did not work out. They were made of vinyl, and because of all the heat still emanating from the rubble, they melted. After that, we switched to a pair made of leather.

We worked sixteen-hour shifts for the next five days. During any "off time," I enjoyed walking outside the secured area and meeting with the local New Yorkers. All were extremely grateful for the efforts of everyone assisting at the site. I've always pictured the typical New Yorker to be a bit crass and self-centered, but that picture soon faded after meeting these people. They were the nicest and most sincere people I have ever met.

During my stay there, Guese had so many "alerts" that I quit counting them. When an alert was made, the area would be marked and members of NYPD Emergency Service Unit along with FDNY and other rescue members would begin the slow process of removing debris until the cause of the alert was found.

I think the people who never got enough credit for the job they did were the ironworkers. These were the people who used cranes, front loaders, and cutting torches, etc., to remove the huge sections of debris for the other workers to gain access. Those people were extremely dedicated and talented.

Throughout my entire stay, we located only body parts. Some were recognizable; most were not. The amount of force with which those buildings came down was absolutely amazing. The destruction was total.

One day after a particularly gruesome find, Guese and I needed to take a break. We walked around the corner to Saint Paul's Episcopal Chapel to reflect. While in the church, a photographer from the Associated Press came in and took our picture. I was not aware that our picture was being taken and vaguely remember someone asking me some questions as I exited the church.

The next day, I received a call from my wife saying that a picture of me sitting on the floor of the church crying was in our local newspaper. As it turned out, newspapers all over the United States and United Kingdom picked up that picture.

After I returned home, I began receiving letters and pictures from all over thanking me for my services. Many were accompanied with little dog treats for Guese. A good majority of them were from schoolchildren. I was extremely humbled to think that these people took the time to write and send their thanks to someone they did not know. The memories of what I saw, heard, felt, and smelled will never be forgotten. It is and will be the most memorable moment of my career.

It was a dark and stormy night. OK, I won't start that way, but it was. Earlier in my shift, an officer had stopped a vehicle for some type of infraction. As the officer approached the vehicle, the driver put it in reverse and attempted to run over the officer. He drove away and was soon out of sight. Three hours later, the vehicle was observed abandoned in a local trailer park. I was called with K-9 Guese to attempt to track the driver. I started Guese at the driver's door of the vehicle.

With his nose to the ground, he began tracking toward a wooded area. It looked like we were on the track of the suspect. Three other backup officers and I followed behind Guese—through the woods, down a steep embankment, across a road, and into a bean field. About fifty yards into the bean field, Guese raised his head and began air-scenting.

To an experienced K-9 handler, this usually indicates that you are getting fairly close to your suspect and to be prepared. Guese led us to an outbuilding of a farm. He air-scented and pulled very hard to the door of the building.

Suspecting that the bad guy was attempting to hide inside the building, we took up positions on the perimeter. I opened the door, gave three loud warnings: "Speak to me now, or I will send the dog." After getting no response from inside, I released Guese to locate and apprehend the suspect. After only a few moments, I could hear some movement from inside. Listening closer I could hear some low growls, followed by some more movements, and even a little whining. Not wanting to rush in and expose ourselves to any hidden dangers, we waited a while longer.

Finally, after not hearing much more noise, we entered the building. We scanned around the first room and saw nothing. Entering the second room, I utilized my flashlight and could see Guese and another dog. Guese was mounted on top of the other dog and doing what dogs do when mounted on each other. No amount of verbal commands was going to get him to stop at that moment.

As it turned out, the farmer owned a large female coon dog. She had come into heat, and the farmer had put her inside the outbuilding to keep unwanted male dogs from coming to visit. I'm sure he never suspected the police would bring their own dog and open the door for him. After Guese and the lovely coon dog finished their date, I spoke to the farmer and explained the situation. Luckily, he saw the humor in it and did not complain. Just goes to show you that even the most highly trained police dog is still . . . just a dog.

K-9 Guese was retired in January 2003 and replaced by K-9 Yogi. I was at home one afternoon when my phone rang. It was the communications center requesting a K-9 not far from my home. A police officer had been dispatched to the local grocery store on a report of a person attempting to pass stolen checks.

The responding officer arrived and confronted the suspect in the parking lot. As the officer was gathering information from the suspect, the suspect struck the officer and fled on foot. It was later determined that the vehicle the suspect had arrived in was stolen.

There was crack cocaine in the car along with numerous stolen checks. The suspect had warrants for his arrest. The officer requested a K-9 to attempt to locate the suspect.

Upon my arrival with K-9 Yogi, we started a track in the area where the officer had last seen the suspect. The track led us into a very thick brush area where most of my movements were by crawling. After only about thirty yards into the track, Yogi located one of the suspect's tennis shoes. Thirty yards later, we located his second shoe. The track led down to a creek where we could see fresh bare footprints in the mud.

Crossing the creek, we continued through a soybean field, two fence rows, through a wooded area, and finally to the banks of the Little Miami River. Fresh footprints again could be seen in the mud on the riverbanks. Because the river was fairly deep and the backup officers and I did not want to get wet, we had another officer with a car pick us up to take us around to the other side of the river.

We began the track again crossing a bike trail and a road. The track led us up a hill where there was very thick brush on our left and a busy highway on our right. Yogi began air-scenting in the area of thick brush, and I was certain that the suspect was in that area. I knew there were other officers on foot, so I could not release the dog. As we got to the top of the hill, there was an intersection.

I could hear someone running through the brush. The suspect popped out of the brush about forty feet from us and initially stopped. I told him to get on the ground or I would send my dog. He hesitated, looked across the road and back at us, then began to run. Yogi apprehended him just as he was jumping over the guardrail.

Yogi's body hit the guardrail on the way down, but he did not let go. After they hit the ground, the suspect stated that he was giving up. After handcuffing the suspect, I gave Yogi the command to let go. The suspect later stated to the officers, "You would never have gotten me if it weren't for that dog!" I do believe he was right.

In 2003, I was attending a K-9 seminar in Tavares, Florida. Along with me were three other dog handlers from our local training group. One of the officers had a jet-black German shepherd. He also happened to be quite good at practical jokes. One day, we decided it was his turn. We got one of the instructors to take that officer to another part of the training facility and keep him occupied for a while.

We went to his cruiser and got his dog out. We took a bottle of white shoe polish and painted a white stripe down the dog from the tip of his nose to the tip of his tail. We put him back into his cruiser and returned to class.

About an hour later, we were all instructed to get our dogs and bring them to the building to do some chemical munitions training. Many officers and instructors had heard about the job we had done and were milling around the parking lot when he got his dog out. The look on his face was priceless. On the other end of his leash was a ninety-pound skunk!

The shoe polish would not wash out and took about three months before it faded. I can only imagine what people were thinking when this officer was walking his dog around their car checking for drugs.

Deputy Sergeant Gene Pence

Ashland County Sheriff's Office, Ashland, Ohio
K-9s Carlos and Ani

Our family was visiting the Ashland County Fair. My eighteen-month-old grandchild had just finished an ice cream cone. I saw a deputy and his dog sitting on the grass beside his cruiser. I asked if we could meet his dog. With permission, Amanda ran up to pet K-9 Ani, who greeted her by licking the ice cream off Amanda's face. That was the beginning of a long friendship. I often rode on patrols with Gene and Ani, watching Gene as he changed roles as volunteer firefighter to EMT, to dive-rescue, and back to patrolling. Often he was the first responder to an accident or fire. We went with sirens and flashing lights.

I did not come from a police family. Back in high school, I wanted to be a fireman. My best friend's dad was working part-time in the sheriff's office. I wanted a job like that. I had to choose, sheriff's deputy or firefighter? I joined the fire department part-time and have been working both ever since. I don't have a job; I have an adventure.

My first K-9 was Carlos, he became known as one of Ashland's most well-known crime fighters. I had to retire him due to a disabling back injury.

Then K-9 Ani became my partner. It is different to have a female K-9. She can sense when I am upset, she will bring her head through the screen opening in the back and lay her head on my shoulder. She will be very still and keep looking at me to see if I am all right. If I have to correct her, it is so different from Carlos. She will cower and look so guilty.

Police dogs are chosen to fit both the officer and the officer's family that the dog will live with. Our county dogs are friendly unless you make an aggressive move toward one of their handlers. One of the main jobs a K-9 does is to protect his officer. He takes this seriously. Our dogs will often be with citizens, so they need to be friendly. When my shift ends,

Ani becomes a family dog. She loves the attention of the neighborhood children.

I mostly do patrolling. I am also the community policing officer. I serve warrants and civil papers, and I run radar. The highway patrol often asks for our help. If they suspect or see drugs, we are called to bring our dogs.

My best friend is Captain Carl Richert. He has K-9 Pitt. Carl says that Pitt knows everything, and Carl is just the student. Despite repeated questioning to Pitt, he did not respond to let me know how well Carl was responding to Pitt's training!

Ani and Pitt play together like puppies. If the two patrol cars are out together, Ani will stick her head out of the window to catch Pitt's scent, then whine and cry for him.

Pitt has his head out of the car in the lead. His scent comes back to her from the open window ahead. Our dogs love to play, but once we give them commands, they immediately become different dogs. Both are extremely well trained. They love kids. They are gentle dogs when the situation calls for that and not so gentle when the situation calls for that.

It is a felony to assault a police officer, and that also covers assaulting a police dog or a police equestrian. Having a police dog is like carrying a gun. It is a tool you hope you will never have to use, but it is there if you need it. Most criminals when confronted with a dog will surrender immediately.

For the well-trained dog, all is a game with the reward of chasing a ball. Dogs chosen for police work need to have a high and hard ball drive; this is described as simply making the dog crazy for his ball or another toy. Out of five or ten dogs you might find one suited for police work. The rest just belong with a loving family.

A narcotics trained dog must be curious, aggressive, and fast. A bomb dog must be silent and cautious. A narcotics dog is never a bomb dog; the training is entirely different. An officer could search for a lost child all day, but often a dog can find the child in minutes.

When we do demos, the public cannot believe how strong a dog's nose is, more than six hundred times stronger than ours. Crowds cannot fathom that. Many have seen K-9s climb walls or jump over walls on TV in shows like *Cops*, but they still marvel that a K-9 right in their own community can do that if need be. Many think this is very special. Handlers do not think they are special, we know we have a tool we can use and that is different from what the normal police officer has.

I like to watch little children; often they are so shy. They will slowly get the courage to edge up toward Ani. They timidly touch her fur and realize that is not too scary. They giggle and pet her.

Our dogs are trained to apprehend but not to maul a suspect. The job is to get the suspect to the ground and keep them there. The dog will release his bite, bark, and stand over the suspect. If the dog stops barking, the officer will know the suspect is trying to get up to run. The dog will then begin to bite again.

A suspect led us on a fifty-mile pursuit with fourteen cruisers and a helicopter trying to stop him. He wrecked the truck and ran into a wooded area. I sent K-9 Ani on an area search on the path toward the lake. I made the announcement, let her off lead, and she took off. She caught a sniff of him and spun around. She always barks when she finds someone. Ani found him! Yea, Ani! I always praise her over and over to let her know she did a good job. That is the only reward she wants, but I also throw her toy for her to chase.

Rural Ashland is beautiful country with rolling hills full of soybean plants and cornfields. Two boys from out of town stole a car and came down here where they used to live. They came to see a girl. They all went joy riding by driving three-fourths of a mile through a farmer's fully developed cornfield. They circled around and around smashing the corn, causing about $5,000 in damage. The farmer saw them and confronted them. They drove the car into a ditch, jumped out, and took off running.

I got there and let Ani get their scent from their car. City officers backed us up. I let Ani go, off she went, we tried to keep up with her. She ran over a mile through the cornfield into some open bean fields, through another field to a farm. She made a hard right to the farmer's barn where she sat waiting for us to catch up. She had her nose to the ground all the way. I had made my announcement and sent her off; it is just fun for her. That was probably the most memorable moment with her. Not that she had tracked and found a robber or murderer but that she had done the track so picture perfect and then sat down to wait for us. She seemed to say, "Hey, they are in there!"

This has been a growing problem, kids coming into rural areas to joyride through the crops. The kids usually do not have money to pay for the damage and often the farmer does not have insurance for vandalism, so he loses much of his business and a year of hard work.

Not everyone can be a dog handler. There are so many different things we need to do that a normal police officer wouldn't do. It is a very large responsibility. When you decide to have a dog, it sheds a different light on what you do on a day-to-day basis.

You cannot just go out to work your eight-hour shift. There is the daily upkeep of the dog. The constant grooming, the vet, the daily reports, and the ongoing training all add additional responsibility to what an officer normally has to do.

I think you need to be a unique person to handle a dog. K-9s in the city or in rural areas may have different settings, but they are basically the same. In both settings, the dog will sniff to find things and will follow the handler's commands. The commands may sound different, but on the whole every handler is the same—with the similar beliefs and goals. You must consider, too, that your dog will do anything in his power if you tell him to. That is exactly what our dogs do. I hate to think they would give up their life for you, but they will. That is hard to grasp.

I am on the dive team. When I first started, we did it for fun, horsing around. Now I dive for bodies and cars. There is a need for rescue recovery teams. We do continual training. I put an invisible shell around myself when diving for a body. I have found eight bodies. If there is family nearby, I will keep the body underwater, so they do not see. I take it over to the boat and put the body into the boat, where it is put into a body bag. I am very aware of family, and I do respect their feelings.

We do not use cadaver dogs here. If necessary, we can get them from the city. I have been doing this for so long and have seen so many tragedies—gunshots, car wrecks, nasty ones—so many dead bodies that it no longer really fazes me. I work with the medic unit and the fire department, so it only really bothers me when it involves a little kid. I have learned to put up with it like the staff in an ER learns to do. Some officers want nothing to do with that. They tell me to let them know when it is all cleaned up. I jump in and begin to work. I don't take time to think about the unpleasant. It is not something I like to do, but things happen, and I am able to help. I have assisted on Metro Life Flight on occasion.

I know the roads I patrol. I can tell you every crack, every pothole, when we go left or when we go right. There are tactical squads that go on the turnpike looking for dope travelers. They will have a dog working there. Many people think we are profiling people. That is a no-no word. We are not profiling; we are looking at every car we pass or see go by. We look for things that lead us to believe we may need to look a bit more.

There are many variables that make us hot on a car. Something does not seem right; it may begin with a traffic violation or people in the car don't look right. Such as kids in a Mercedes or something just doesn't look right in this situation. We work on that.

If I have reason to stop the car, I do it. I ask questions and see how they answer. Do their answers fit what I see? If they tell me they are going on vacation, but there is nothing in the car, no luggage, it could be in the trunk, but I don't know that. Telltale signs, the demeanor of the persons. Do they look nervous? Some will shake my hand after I give them a ticket, not many, though.

My K-9 Ani, Carl's K-9 Pitt, Lieutenant Deaton and his K-9 Odett, and Wendy with K-9 Aaron make up our K-9 unit. The dogs are considered law enforcement officers. They have a swearing-in ceremony as do the handlers. If someone attacks a police dog, it is the same as assaulting an officer. When they are not on patrol or out training, they are used in jails and courtrooms.

When an inmate is moved from a cell to a courtroom one of the dogs is often put on lead; he will bark and growl all the way to and from the cells. This has eliminated fighting. The inmates know dogs bite; they wish to avoid that.

When I decided to go to assist at the World Trade Center, I did not know what I would do there. I knew I wanted to help where there was the most need. Carl was going, too. We took respirators, gloves, steel-toed boots, plastic suits, and other much needed rescue supplies, all donated by local businesses and residents. We also took several thousand dollars to help with the relief. We just wanted to do anything that was needed to help the people of New York City. We are both trained firefighters as well as law enforcement officers. We are both experienced in rescue extraction.

I had heard that there were more than two hundred K-9s at the site.

So I left Ani at home. I realized my mistake when I got there. There were actually very few K-9 search-and-rescue dogs at the site. We were speechless with what we saw. First we went to Ground Zero and worked with an engine company, working a truck to pump water to the piles that had been Towers One and Two.

Later we worked the K-9 MASH unit, a trauma hospital set up to care for the working dogs. The dogs would come into the triage area with partials stuck between their toes. Their pads had cuts that needed treatment. Most did wear booties to avoid the sharp pieces of steel from the fallen beams. They were often dehydrated and given water. Their noses needed to be cleaned, so they could continue to work. We did anything the dogs needed. We were so busy but felt as though we did so little as so much was needed.

When we returned home, Senator Bill Harris honored us with plaques thanking us for our help.

Training

Julie McHugh

Boston, Massachusetts
K-9 Training Decoy

Julie's motel room was next to mine during a training week in Florida. When you think of someone in a bite suit, you would never think of Julie. She is a tall, willowy, Bostonian lady with a passion for training dogs. One of the training sites was a fire academy. About twenty young fire cadets were supposed to be working on a written assignment; they simply dropped their pencils and watched in disbelief as Julie sat confidently on an upturned milk crate while dog after dog was commanded to GET THAT BAD GUY (Julie). The K-9s attacked her at a full run, knocking her off the crate as they latched their jaws into her bite suit. A bite suit weighs about twenty-five pounds; it is a roomy, slightly bulky, suit of compacted padding meant to hold up under serious abuse, dirt, dog teeth, and dragging on the pavement. It is very warm and cumbersome to wear. Julie does not wear a helmet. Her hands are exposed to being bitten or stepped on by an officer. Another day, she sat in a car with the windows rolled down. Again the dogs were commanded to GET THAT BAD GUY. I watched in disbelief wondering how she could just sit there waiting for a lunging dog to come flying through the open car window to drag her out.

I wear a bite suit and become a decoy as I assist in training dogs. I have been a decoy for both police K-9 handlers and civilian dog handlers for more then eight years. I like to believe I am always mentally and physically prepared to take the hit when the dog is commanded to stop me. Then I deliver as real a fight as possible to the officer coming to assist his dog. I am told I am pretty good. For years, I had walked around with a little *umph*, boosted by the knowledge that a dog has never really bested me.

I would work the scenarios given to me until I met K-9 Ammo. He was a K-9 out of Austin, Texas. He was not exactly handled but more "contained and directed" by Officer Jimmie Davenport. Jimmie is about five foot six to my five foot eleven. We were working high-risk car stops scenarios. We would line up three vehicles—the lead car being an undercover police car, the second car carrying myself with my partner-in-crime driving, followed by a van carrying a SWAT team, including two K-9 teams.

As the lead vehicle comes to a stop sign, my car pulls up behind it. The SWAT truck then rams us forward, jamming our car between two police vehicles. Officers seemed to pour from both cars. A flash-bang distraction device is thrown at both of our doors. My cohort and I then exit the vehicle. My partner "shooting" at the police while I make a break for it. I was running past the first car and then Ammo was sent after me. For safety reasons, Ammo has a four-foot leash trailing from his collar.

As he passed my car, his leash swung under the rear tire stopping the dog midair at thirty-five miles an hour. He slammed into the passenger door. Seeing the horrifying crash, I instinctively reached for the dog. He responded to my concern by leaping and lunging in a fury of frustration. The illustrious K-9 Officer Jimmie Davenport reacted to the whole thing as only a true Southern gentleman could; he calmly approached, reached for the leash and disengaged it, whispering GOOD BOY, GOT THAT BAD GUY, GOOD BOY!

Another run-in with K-9 Ammo and Jimmie happened while teaching the "join your dog in the fight" curriculum. The dog is sent to me but cannot get me to the ground, so the handler must join his dog in an effort to put me down and get me into a cuffing position. We typically run each dog team through this three times: once, to give the officer an idea of how things will go; the second time, to get the dog on board; and finally a full-speed run-through.

The first team up underestimated my commitment to a true-to-life experience. The officer ignored my request to remove his glasses. When it came time for the third run-through, I went full-tilt (accidentally) and caught him upside his face, breaking his glasses. Next up was the team of Jimmie and Ammo.

Having seen what I had just done, I guess Jimmie had decided he wasn't going to suffer the embarrassment of being slapped by a girl decoy. The soft-spoken gentleman sent his dog, crossed behind me, took my free arm, and slammed me to the floor, causing a buzzing sensation as I almost lost consciousness.

Throughout my ordeal, I wore Ammo like a shirtsleeve as he took full advantage of my slightly altered state and busily set about beating me into submission by my left arm. Then Ammo assisted his partner by pulling my outstretched arm down and across my back, handing it to Jimmie's waiting handcuff.

At the end of the day, I still love what I do. There are few things more admirable than dog teams dedicated to one another. There are few teams nobler than the faith and loyalty a handler and his K-9 have for each other. Imagine knowing in your heart that your partner would die for you and knowing at your core that you can trust your dog.

For me, there is no greater rush than "catching dogs." I can tell you it isn't sweating in the heavy, hot bite suit that appeals to me or getting knocked around or even the repeated handcuffing. (What fun!) The rush comes from being one of the greatest impressions on that dog's ego. Send a soft, unsure dog at a well-trained, solid decoy, and that dog can walk away minutes later, confident it can take down mountains.

It can be a ton of fun and a barrel of laughs. One of the funniest moments involved the rocket dog out of Lakeland, Florida. He hit me so high and fast, he took the bite sleeve with him as he sailed over my shoulder in swanlike flight.

One of my all-time favorite bloopers would have to be an ugly episode in my hometown of Boston along the Charles River. (Read: cesspool with a current.) In our efforts to train a hardheaded dog to stop just before the bite and return to his handler, we employed the available resources and hatched what was sure to be an effective correction.

Our plan was to send the dog at me while I stood at the end of a boat dock (can you see this coming?), and when he didn't stop, I would step out of his path, thus landing him in the slime cocktail that is the Charles River. Remember, I said this dog was hardheaded!

As the dog passed by me, airborne, he twisted toward me grabbing the slightest hold on my sleeve and gracefully pulled me, my bite suit, and my cell phone backward into the brownish-green water.

God, I love this job!

In another session, the handler sends the dog to stop me just before he hits me with a bite. I turn and yell, *"No hablo inglés. estoy embarrassada, estoy embarrassada!"* Translation is "I cannot speak English, I'm pregnant, I'm pregnant!" This has got to be the single most frustrating exercise a dog is put through. We finished that training, having annoyed all the dogs present. The team met in the hotel parking lot to plan where to go for lunch. A straggling handler came out of his room; his dog was off leash. He announced, "Loose dog," as is considered proper etiquette.

About four seconds later, the dog approached our group, sniffed around, and realized that I, his sorely missed quarry, was right there. Four hours and thirty-six stitches later in the emergency room, I was back on my feet, though very embarrassed. I was now wearing a skirt so as not to rub my sore hindquarters unnecessarily.

I suspect the dog has a tally somewhere totaling up all the butt cheeks he has sunk his teeth into. Imagine the graphic he might use. Can I get a side of humiliation with that, please?

Let me take a moment to define my purpose in lending my time and efforts to these ventures. I, at the time, was thirty-four with six years working with law enforcement officers and sixteen years working with dogs in all capacities.

I love the animal. I love its set of standards of behavior and its polar abilities of true care and concern versus total base survival instinct. While I have met law enforcement K-9s I did not like, I have never met one I did not respect. Amazing this animal we call on for companionship, defense, aggression, obedience, and loyalty. They often come closer to us than siblings or spouses. Amazing. When someone will ask why I do this, I always say—for the dog!

Dog Handler Michael Cleverley

Ministry of Defence Guard Service, Portsmouth, England
K-9 LUGER

Mick came to the United States to bring well-trained K-9 Luger for a deputy with the Worcester County Sheriff's Office in Maryland. Mick did not have use of a car, so I was able to drive him from his hotel each morning to the different training sites. He worked with the local Maryland handlers as a trainer. When he returned home, he sent me a shepherd dog carved from a piece of coal. He told me that his father, grandfather, and many uncles had all worked in the mines in Northumberland. His joy was contagious as a first-time visitor to our country.

I qualified as a dog handler in 1987, having passed the British military dog handlers' course with the Royal Army Veterinarian Corps (RAVC) based in Melton Mowbray, Leicestershire, which is now known as the Defence Animal Centre. It trains service and civilian personnel dog-handling skills, also service dogs for active duty around the world, including all the various different breeds used for patrol dogs, guard dogs, drug detection, and arms and explosives.

I have competed in many service dog trials over the years as a Ministry of Defence dog handler. During my career, I have been teamed with five GSD (German shepherd dogs) patrol dogs trained in attack work, to patrol and secure military establishments here in the United Kingdom.

My passion is working my four English springer spaniels—training and breeding gundogs for the field. I also correct and retrain problem dogs. I am currently a member of the British Institute of Professional Dog Trainers, Hampshire Gundog Society, and the English Springer Spaniel Club.

It all started in September 2001.While training a GSD named Luger for security work here in the United Kingdom. One of my friends owned a private security company. He exported trained dogs for various police roles.

He asked if I wanted to travel with him and two dogs to do a handover with the new K-9 handlers. Then we would carry out his basic training. That included leashed and unleashed obedience. I groomed him to form a bond before starting out on the criminal training after seven days.

We then introduced the padded sleeve used as protection for the criminal (myself to wear) while doing attack work. This involves building up the dog's courage to attack and hold on to a fleeing criminal until given a release command. Also to defend his handler from any aggressor. This involves the dog being able to detect an intruder, using his scenting to indicate to his handler either by scent or sight or hearing, and leading the handler to the said person. This is done over a period of time with small training exercises, with the dog kept on a long training lead.

Luger thrived on all the attack work. After completing various set laid-down stages, he was soon completing the attack of the lead on—what we call a "full trip." He was taught to restrain the person by biting and holding on to the right arm, until called off by his handler. He had to be willing to re-attack without any commands on any aggression shown towards the dog's handler.

During this time, the dog had been sold to the Worcester County Sheriff's Office, to be reteamed with Deputy Calvin Purnell as his new K-9 partner.

A week prior to leaving the United Kingdom, both dogs went to the vets for export documentation to be completed along with health inspections for import. I was happy both dogs passed with flying colors.

In January 2002, all the travel arrangements had been made for the trip. The two dogs were to be crated and fly as cargo on the way out. We loaded up the vehicles at around 0800 and set off for Gatwick Airport, about a sixty-five-mile drive, for the start of a new working career for GSD Luger, and a black Lab drug dog called Charlie.

We landed at Dulles Airport, Washington, D.C., to be met by all the customs officers, so along with the dogs we went through immigration. Our passports were checked; important documentation and veterinarian health papers for both dogs all checked.

After entering the arrivals lounge, the fun started, I had Luger in a large wooden crate on a luggage trolley, all marked up: CAUTION, POLICE DOGS, WILL BITE. And he was just a little bit boisterous by now, barking and growling and jumping about in his crate at all the people in the area. He had spent too many hours locked up during transport. People kept coming up to ask if they were real dogs inside the crates; this just made him worse. Many times the crate fell off the trolley.

Then we met a posse of police officers anxiously waiting to meet their new partners. So off we went, outside to the car park, so the dogs could be given a short walk and toilet break, before starting off on another car journey to our final destination.

The following week was carried out putting Luger through various training scenarios with Deputy Calvin Purnell, Worcester County Sheriff's Office. Luger had not been fully trained yet for operational duties. We started off conducting the next stage of his training—introduction to tracking and drugs indication—all of which the dog took in his stride.

This is when I was introduced to the author Joan and her loving husband, Bob, who took us under their wing and escorted us to the various training grounds. When we do any sort of bite work, the "baiter" or "catcher"—or as you call them, "decoy"—will start to moan and groan to add a bit of reality. The first time I was working as decoy to agitate Luger, Joan thought I had been hurt because of the squealing I was doing.

We also visited one of the prison correction centers to watch Charlie do his stuff working around various vehicles on drug work with his new handler. The senior officer came out to watch the training program and was very impressed with the dog after only being teamed for a few days. We watched all the officers from the prison putting their dogs through various search scenarios.

The week's training ended at around midday on the Friday, concluding with an official handover of GSD Luger to Deputy Calvin Purnell and a media shoot for the local papers.

Constable Maurice (Mo) Parry
Delta Police Department, Delta, British Columbia, Canada
K-9 Decoy

Mo is often the decoy with Bob Eden's training teams. He is a quiet, behind-the-scenes man. I watched him often take time to listen and help any handler who had a problem with his dog. When he is at home in Canada, he is part of the police emergency response team.

My dad was a Royal Canadian Mounted Police officer. Mum was a dispatcher for 911 Delta Police Department. I used to drive by her work after high school to do my homework or just to see her. As a result, I got to know some of the officers. It wasn't long before I met Bob Eden.

Being young and foolish, I quickly volunteered. He gave me a bite sleeve. I was fifteen years old; the padded sleeve was half the size I was. He told me to run down the street to a church, go in the back, and hide in the bushes. He said, "Just hunker down and wait. When you see me coming with my dog, jump out of the bushes and start running. I am going to send the dog after you. All you have to do is to keep the sleeve between you and the dog."

All right. I ran down the street and hid in the bushes behind the church. I had never seen police dog training or participated in it. I was sitting there, and my mind was racing wondering what I should expect. Then I saw the dog coming.

My heart began to go thump. *Oh man, that is a big black police dog!* I got up and started running for all I was worth. Bob had let the dog go and it came running after me. The adrenaline rush was through the roof. The dog latched onto the sleeve. I thought, *This wasn't as scary as I thought it would be.* It was actually quite a lot of fun. The adrenaline rush was fun, and the chase was fun.

Bob invited me to regular training at the police department every Thursday night. I did that all through high school. All my close friends knew; they also knew I came from a police family. My best friend also helped train for years as well. Another close friend also had a dad in the Delta police, but not everyone shared the same interest in being chased by a police dog as I did.

It was not always fun and games. I also laid some of the track that could be boring and monotonous. The bread and butter of police dog work is tracking. That is not always exciting. I liked the bite work and practicing high-risk auto stops.

I still enjoyed it and knew at an early age that I wanted to be a police officer. I set my goal to become a Delta police officer and eventually a dog handler. That is exactly what I did. I took criminal courses at the university. When I was eighteen, I volunteered for the Citizens' Crime Watch Patrol. I started washing police cars for a part-time summer job and volunteered at the community police station. I was volunteering in different areas of law enforcement. I was very focused at a very young age; I knew what I was going to do. Very goal-focused. I was hired at twenty-one; I worked very hard and did very well during a time when the hiring was mainly females and minorities, not young white men.

I was in the right place at the right time. When I became First-Class Constable, I could apply for the specialties departments. I applied for the dog section and got it.

I got Bob Eden's car, his call sign, and some of his equipment, and the pressure and responsibility of being a K-9 handler. Could I be relied upon by the patrol officers and the management and the community? There was a lot of pressure, and there still is to this day.

I have been very fortunate to work with Bob as well as Brian Helm, former head trainer for the Calgary Police Department. I have been able to work with two of the top professionals for a number of years as a decoy and handler.

My expertise is as a decoy. The role of the decoy is extremely important for younger dogs (or earlier stages of dog training). Any fool can put on a padded sleeve and take a bite, but it takes a sophisticated individual who understands animal behavior, someone who is able to read a dog's behavior, and be able to respond to it and manipulate behavior. A good decoy can build up a dog's confidence.

What we want to build in our police dogs is not a frenzied dog who is like a loose cannon running around biting everyone and everything. Our dogs are professional athletes. To be a good decoy can take years. Very few people know this. The best sport dogs, the best street dogs, had handlers with access to people decoys capable of manipulating dogs' behavior and bringing out the best in the dog.

The contact many police officers have with the public is not always positive. The average contact a citizen has with law enforcement is a traffic stop. The citizen is not pulled over to be praised for his good driving. It is often a negative incident. For us to deal with a lot of crap and shit, it means so much for someone to tell us thank you for doing a good job.

I love my job! If I did not like it, I would not be doing it. I do not do this as a means of existence, but because I have a passion for it. I also enjoy being part of Bob Eden's police K-9 conferences as part of the team. I help teach K-9 officers all types of situations that they will likely encounter on the streets. We teach a tactical safe way of training.

Andrew Rebmann

Connecticut State Police Officer, Retired
Seattle, Washington
Coauthor of *Cadaver Dog Handbook*

Andy coauthored Cadaver Dog Handbook: Forensic Training *and* Tactics for the Recovery of Human Remains *with Edward David. Any time cadaver dog training was mentioned, Andy's name kept popping up. I wanted to meet the master. I met Andy and his wife, Marcia Koenig, in a small restaurant called Saigon Rose outside of Seattle, Washington. Andy told me he has participated in over a thousand dog searches. They also hold classes to train search-and-rescue teams, cadaver dogs, and disaster training.*

When I got my first K-9 patrol dog, our department required a two-year commitment for me to become a handler. I figured I would do that and then get into the detective bureau. When I retired eighteen years later, I was still handling dogs, except by then I had two shepherds and two bloodhounds.

A new handler has to learn that having a dog does not just mean that you now get to take a cruiser home and have a dog to play with. Now you suddenly have a lot of extra work. I don't know how many times my supervisor said, "You look like a slob with all that dog hair on your uniform." That was back in the days before we wore specialty uniforms. The wool pants on the old uniforms would collect the hair from the German shepherds. You also have a car to keep clean; there are always nose prints on the windows and hair everywhere.

My first patrol shepherd was 105 pounds, extremely impressive, with a very hard bite. I was outside of my car when I saw a guy trying to put his kid's hand into the back window to pet the patrol dog.

If it had been an adult, my dog would have eaten him! But since it was a little kid, the dog did nothing. I told that guy exactly what I thought of him. In Connecticut, we do not paint ourselves into a lawsuit.

I had my vehicle rigged so I could carry two bloodhounds and one shepherd or two shepherds and one bloodhound. I had all the equipment I needed. I drove a Suburban with crates in the back. You would not want to put your hand in my vehicle.

I was working a case of a missing boy. A TV reporter decided to stick his camera lens into the back of my Suburban. The bloodhound very nicely crunched it. The reporter did not appreciate that.

We hold training classes around the country. We have many searches, not only for cadavers but also for lost children and Alzheimer's patients. One of the dogs in our unit has had three finds lately. He found a lady stuck in the mud in a little lake. The lady was holding herself up but was becoming hypothermic. Another few hours and she might not have been able to continue to hold herself above the mud. She had been with a friend tubing or floating on the Green River when they became disoriented and ended up in a hazardous spot. The man took a quart of beer and went for help. He was too intoxicated to give instructions on where he had left his friend. Our dog found her.

It is a constant battle to educate people how to handle a scene if you are running behind a tracking dog. The handler must learn to protect the scene and not let people muddle it up. If you are doing a building search with a bad guy inside, first secure the perimeter and then let the dog do the work.

Search-and-rescue groups were started here in King County, Washington, in the late 1960s. Here the K-9 handlers act as search-and-rescue deputies. When we go on searches, the police know how our dogs work. They will do the tracking when going after a bad guy. But they turn the missing persons over to us. We have a nice working relationship. Washington State Law prohibits any volunteer going after a criminal suspect. Or if someone reports a missing person who has left a note— and the missing person is suicidal with a gun—they will not send us. The police take care of that. We are prohibited from taking part in any criminal activity as we could not take the appropriate action as volunteers.

Our training classes for search and rescue are very hard. A volunteer has to pay for the classes and ours are not inexpensive. Some come with a dog that is nothing more then a cement block on the end of a leash.

There are some dogs that I could work with for seven days a week doing basic tracking and basic cadaver search—and certain dogs still could not find their handler in a telephone booth. I have to tell that person his or her dog is not suited for this job. I know this because the dog does not have the basic drive necessary to complete the job. We have to let the volunteers make their own mistakes. It is not an easy decision for them. Sometimes they will bring a second or third dog. It can be a difficult situation.

We drove up to Snohomish to help search for a missing boy. It took two hours in traffic to get there, only to find the boy had been found hidden in a cardboard box. He thought it was funny to have everyone looking for him. We have had kids sneak back into their house when we had a full search going.

Working with volunteers is hard, at times even trying, but it is very rewarding. They become like family. Now we have friends around the world. Many of the volunteers we have taught went to the World Trade Center to help. Marcia was there to do paperwork as part of the mortuary team. It was a pleasure to work again with people she had helped train.

Sometimes a former student will say, "My dog did something different, and in training you had told me to always check that out. You were so right." On searches, you never know what you will find. On a live search, the dogs are trained to go to the live subject and go back to the handler to let him know of the find.

One day, we were working on a hill near an elementary school. Near it was a chain link fence. On the other side of the fence were blackberry bushes. The dog just stopped and stared. He did not bark and did not indicate a find; he just stared. If your dog does something different, you should always investigate to see why. The handler called and to her surprise the suspect answered. The dog could not reach the suspect, so he did not alert in the usual way. You cannot always expect a trained alert. It doesn't always happen.

A dog to be trained for search and rescue needs to have a bit of maturity and be about nine or ten months of age. You hope you can work the dog for eight to ten years. Shepherds are very susceptible to spinal arthritis. The trainer has to gage the physical capability of each. The training procedure is mainly a mechanical operation. We have held classes in many states. We teach cadaver searches and trailing for Alzheimer's patients. We also do disaster training.

To reward my dog, I keep a tennis ball in my pocket. When she has found the victim, she runs back to me and puts her nose by that pocket and then will run back to show me where the victim is. The only reward she wants is praise and time to play with a dirty old tennis ball.

I had a difficult situation when I retired my first patrol dog. All of a sudden, as I put on my uniform, I had to tell my dog he could not go to work with me but the new dog was going. There were not too many face-offs between them, as the older one gradually became accustomed to staying home and being a house dog.

Over the years, I trained and worked with both German shepherds and bloodhounds:

K-9s Tina, Clem, Rufus, Josie, Lady, and Marianne. My male bloodhounds were mostly friendly rivals. Marcia's dog was Coyote, she was an alpha female with a very high drive. She would have been a great police dog with her energy. Some dogs retire themselves. They have worked hard and have decided they do not want to work anymore. Both of our dogs worked until the week before they died.

Dottie Danko

Wife of Lieutenant John Danko
Shaker Heights Police Department, Shaker Heights, Ohio

I attended the Shaker Heights Citizens Police Academy. Officers from different departments would speak at our evening classes. One night, Dottie spoke to us in a very honest way to let us know what it is like to be the wife of an officer, especially the wife of a sniper on the SWAT team. Dottie is a registered nurse, a very soft-spoken woman.

I met John when we were both in the air force. We had dated a few times when I asked him what he planned to do when his enlistment was up. He thought for a few minutes and said, "I want to be a police officer. If you don't like that, it is too bad." I didn't know why he said that; it wasn't as though I was going to marry him or something. In those days, it was not very popular to be a police officer.

We did get married some thirty years ago. It has been a roller-coaster ride. John always made a point of telling me about his day when he got home. If it had been a very rough day, he might wait a day or two. I knew when to leave him alone. But other times, I would keep after him to get him to talk. Communication is so very important in any marriage, but even more so in a police family. Many officers try to keep stress to themselves, but we do not. I am not a chatterbox, but I do agree that communication is the key to a good lasting relationship.

I wish I could tell you that there is a secret ingredient to being a good wife, but there isn't. We just share our concerns, our fears, our joys, and our ambitions. John has told me never to leave him on a negative note. Sometimes that is difficult. If that happens, he will call me at work or I will phone him.

An officer seems to go through at least three stages. The first one is the hotdog stage when he believes that he is bullet-proof, that he can knock down walls, that he can get the bad guy no matter what stands in the way. John calls that the "John Wayne" syndrome.

Then after witnessing so many terrible things, an officer may go into the loner stage, believing that the whole world is full of terrible people and terrible things. Often they do not convey their feelings to their spouses or anyone. They only want to associate with fellow officers. They isolate themselves.

At this point, John had seen one murder after another; he had seen children being used as ashtrays with cigarette burns all over them. It was hard not to be disgusted with the world. That was a trouble spot for us. We were not talking about the problems.

We knew we had to talk. John even said he regretted being a police officer; he felt he had taken the wrong test. There is a spirit of good-natured kidding between police officers and firefighters. When a police officer gets depressed, he wishes he had taken the firefighters' test. He sees everyone loving a firefighter, while cops are not as lucky. Later, when our daughter married a firefighter, we had a good laugh.

John had assisted at many drug busts with drug dealers heavily into the scene. He began to be very aware of our surroundings and wanted our daughter and me to also be very aware. I had to drive her to school and pick her up. He told me of an officer who had been on drug busts. That officer had gone to school to pick up his young child. She was on the play-ground swing being pushed by the drug dealer! Message given. "I know where you live. I know where to find you. Lay off me!" To this day, John insists I check my surroundings. I am never to enter a building without first looking in the window to see if it seems normal. Is there someone inside with their arms raised?

We always sit in the back of a restaurant with John's back to the wall, so he can see the doorway. I had not known that anyone who really wanted my address or phone number could find it. We were never totally safe. I do not like to sound paranoid, but there is no reason to walk into trouble if you don't have to. Most citizens go around with blinders on.

Besides communication, I would advise wives to go on ride-alongs with other officers. They would see the drudgery, the reports, and the ugliness, and realize how important it is to talk about that each day. They would see what happens on a shift, there is good as well as the ugly. They would see the pressures as well as the joking and friendships that run deeply between many officers.

The best advice I could give future brides would be to ride along on a shift, ask questions, and then see if you and your intended can talk about important things. If there is a problem, solve it before marriage. Don't fall in love with the uniform but rather the personality of the man.

Later we moved to another police department, one that is family-oriented. Suddenly, there were police family picnics. Families could shoot on the range and go on ride-alongs.

John came into the third stage excited and confident of being a police officer. We still talk every day about what has happened that day. It was a great help to us as a couple to begin dating before John was a police officer. Many young ladies seem to fall in love with the glamour of the uniform.

Some police marriages have ended in less then a month. Being a police officer can change a person. A new wife should understand that her husband might go through many different stages. If they do not talk she may feel this "new" person he has become may be permanent.

The third stage is a truly confident officer enjoying his job, able to talk about horrible things in his work with his wife. Many still do not trust another person to help. Most times, a wife can help if she will be patient and listen. This has been a good life. I cannot complain.

Robert S. Eden

Handler and Trainer, Delta Police Department
Delta, British Columbia, Canada
Author of *Dog Training for Law Enforcement*
and *K-9 Officer's Manual*

Bob is president of Eden Consulting Group, a business comprised of police officers dedicated to the training of police K-9 handlers. The training sessions are called International K-9 Conferences. I was invited to observe two weeks with the team in Tavares, Florida. Bob would tell me each day what I would be observing; later he explained what each session taught the handlers. I guess I did not listen carefully to the instructions on the gas house. The handlers with gas masks had their dogs on short leads as they lined up to go inside to find and apprehend the "suspect." I stood off to one side. Suddenly, the breeze changed directions and my lungs had a gulp of gas. The gas did not seem to bother the dogs at all. As they exited, the handlers would give the dogs drinks of water and wash their fur with a hose. At the end of the two weeks of twelve-hour training days, I sat in an observation platform overlooking the shooting range. Ten or more officers were shooting at targets at the same time. There was the loud sound of continuous gunfire and the ping-ping of targets being hit, officers yelling commands, and dogs barking. This made for a wonderful ending. Suddenly, a helicopter flew overhead with bright lights shining on the activity below. I looked at Bob and said, "Well, what is planned for tomorrow?"

As working on the streets becomes more dangerous to the officers and the citizens we protect, we must keep abreast of the most versatile and successful techniques available to us. Our goal is to provide those techniques to the handlers and support them by providing the most effective and ethical service possible to their community.

The public must be aware that the vast majority of law enforcement officers are both moral and ethical. As K-9 handlers, we do hold ourselves to a higher standard. We work hard under immense stress. It is a violent world and as law enforcement we are always at risk.

Training like ours is what every officer should have on a regular basis. The officers will have less risk of getting injured on the job when they go through regular intensive training. At the end of two weeks of training the officers are given a performance evaluation sheet to fill out. The interesting word that often appears is "passion." They tell us the instructors were passionate about the training and really cared about the officers and the dogs. Each of our instructors has at least fifteen years as an experienced police officer working with dogs.

In our training, we teach morals and ethics as they relate to police work in general. You can do something that is legal and be entirely within legal bounds to do it as a police officer or a citizen. That does not mean it fits within what society expects from you.

Many people can do things that are probably not the right way to deal with things and yet be legally capable of doing them. The problem of doing that is you bring yourself down to a level that is less than what you should be as a police officer, particularly one who has the ability to use force on a daily basis, and particularly with the use of a police dog.

The vast majority use their dogs solely for the purpose of a search tool, and very seldom is the dog used as a weapon. It does happen that a dog is needed to apprehend somebody, but not all the time. I want the people we teach to come across as very, very professional.

I want them to be morally sound in making the right decisions for the right reasons. They need to think things through before acting, so the deployment of the dog is done for the right reason. If you can do something by using less force, then it is incumbent upon us to use less force.

We must use dogs in a very judicious way. We do not want to be sending the dogs out to make apprehensions every time there is an opportunity. We must have the legal capability when we have a suspect who has fled from a crime scene. If the suspect is hiding and I cannot see his hands, I can legally send my dog. I still want to give him every opportunity to give up before I have to do that—as long as it does not put others or me in potential jeopardy.

I know for a fact that the citizens need to trust that I am not out there abusing my dog or my position as a police officer.

The times ahead will be troubled times in the law enforcement community. Police dog applications are a particularly favorite target of the civil liberty agencies throughout the United States at this point in time.

It is up to police officers to maintain a level of professionalism that will protect all of us from those who seek to restrict K-9 work in law enforcement. As working the streets becomes more of a danger to the officers and the citizens we must protect, there are those who are constantly trying to strip us of any physical, mental, or spiritual security we now have as police officers.

We cannot allow that to happen. Regardless of what training or apprehension methods we might adhere to, the time has come for all agencies to come together and work toward a common goal. The goal should be to provide the most effective and ethical service possible to the community in which we work. This cannot be done on continual restricted budgets. We will need the support of police administrations around the country if it is to succeed. Being a police officer is difficult because you see so much bad stuff; there is so much negative in the world.

A few years ago the headlines read: "Deputy Matt Williams and his K-9 Dioji were shot and killed in Lakeland, Florida. Deputy Williams of Polk County was responding as backup for a colleague who had stopped the assailant for speeding." Matt and his K-9 Dioji had been one of the teams participating in our two-week training session.

This was a very sad event for everyone. Our instructors remembered Matt from training. When we heard about this incident, we were just finishing another training week in Modesto, California, so the news came hard to our team. Yet it reinforced to us that we need to continue what we are doing. This certainly validates everything that we as trainers do to try to teach these officers how to be safe on the street. Sadly, regardless how much we train and prepare for the job, the risk will always remain high. Every dog handler, every police officer, knows the risk and like any soldier in the field, every single one without exception is willing to take that risk.

Made in the USA
Columbia, SC
19 January 2018